Lapize: now there was an ace

Jean Bobet

Lapize:
now there was an ace

Translated by Adam Berry

LAPIZE: NOW THERE WAS AN ACE

English edition first published in 2010

by:

Mousehold Press
Victoria Cottage
Constitution Opening
Norwich NR3 4BD

www.mousehold-press.co.uk

Originally published in France by La Table Ronde,
under the title *Lapize; celui-là était un 'as'*

Cover design: Terence Loan

All photographs from the author's personal collection

ISBN 978 1 874739 55 5

CONTENTS

When it comes to people we have known, we do not attach ourselves to those who have died, we attach them to ourselves. Everyone is convinced that he knows the departed better than anyone else.
Antoine Blondin

Introduction to the French edition

In the early 1950s, my brother Louison and I were living in the Eastern suburbs of Paris. Whenever we went training, we would cycle past the Café Lapize in Villiers-sur-Marne. This Lapize seemed to follow us everywhere. At the time, Lapize toe straps were the only ones on the market. At the Montlhéry motor racing circuit there was the famous slope known as the Côte Lapize, which determined the outcome of every race held there.

Back in Villiers-sur-Marne, you couldn't find Octave Lapize at the café any more. We knew he had been killed in the war, the 1914-18 one. People even said he died a hero.

The Café Lapize belonged to the champion's father. One day, I ducked under the arbour at the entrance and went inside. Across the large room, I came face to face with the great Octave Lapize, in a large pastel drawing on the wall, resplendent in his French champion's tricolour jersey. I was looking at the portrait of a true aristocrat. An inscription underneath read 'Winner of the Tour de France, Paris-Roubaix (three times), Paris-Brussels (three times).'

I spent fifty years thinking about Octave Lapize. Then, one day, I decided to follow his tracks and tell his story. Thanks to him, I experienced the golden age of cycling at the beginning of the twentieth century. The Lapize years.

Jean Bobet

FOREWORD

What was his first name, again?

Octave.

Oh yes, Octave. Octave Lapize…

And that was it.

My grandmothers, who were about the same age as him, used to say that he went past quickly, that Octave Lapize. Not yet thirty. And once he had gone past, he disappeared.

However, for some reason it seems to me that I have always known him. I have traced him back to his own territory in Villiers-sur-Marne; I have touched him at the end of the straps, bearing his name, that secured my toe clips. I have looked for him at the top of the Côte Lapize at the Montlhéry circuit; I have imagined him in the cockpit of his Nieuport plane in the sky over Lorraine.

One day last year, I found him sitting on a sofa and immediately recognized his mop of curly hair and the mischievous glint in his eye. After a conversation lasting two hours, the voice from the sofa gently interrupted me to ask how I knew all this, and why I wanted to talk about it all.

But I should confess.

The voice from the sofa was not that of Octave, who had long since disappeared. It belonged to his daughter Yvonne, who had never really made an appearance.

7

Dear Yvonne Lapize-Lambert, please allow me to offer you the pages that follow. In remembrance of your father, the champion and hero whose tracks I have followed wherever they left a trace.

Yvonne, in her father's arms, 1916.

A LIFE OF THIRTY YEARS
(in extracts)

Extract from a birth certificate drawn up by us, Philippe Laziès, Mayor, Civil Officer of State of the XIVth *arrondissement* of Paris. October 1887.

> *In the year eighteen hundred and eighty seven, on the twenty-sixth day of October at a quarter to one: This is to certify the birth of Louis Octave Lapize, male, born on the twenty-fourth of this month at six o'clock in the evening at the residence of his father and mother, number 49 rue Bénard.*

Extract from the *Encyclopédie des Coureurs Français* sponsored by the French Cycling Federation, 1998 :

Octave LAPIZE

Amateur career

French cyclo-cross champion

French 100-kilometre champion

Third place in the 100-kilometre race at the London Olympic Games

Holder of the world motor-paced hour record

Etc.

Professional career

French Champion

Winner, Tour de France

Winner, Paris–Roubaix

Winner, Paris–Tours

Winner, Paris–Brussels

Winner, Milan–Varèse

Winner, Brussels Six Days

World track record-holder

Etc.

Extract from a letter written by Air Force Sergeant Boillot, July 1917:

Good old Octave Lapize, stationed with N90 Squadron, 20 kilometres away at Toul, came to visit us at N77 on 12 July. He cycled over, making use of the bad weather to keep himself in training, he said. He left us in the evening, full of beans, and our last sight of old Lapize was of a figure bent over his handlebars as he sped up the hill with no apparent effort, and disappeared over the top. That was the last chance we were given to admire the hero.

A telephone call at eight o'clock on Saturday 14 July broke the news of the irrevocable tragedy.

AT THAT TIME

At that time, around 1910, France was making the unwitting transition from the Belle Époque to the pre-war period.

At that time, war's distant thunder could already be heard. Russia was measuring up to Austro-Hungary, and France to Germany, but it was all happening in the Balkans and Morocco. Parliament was buzzing, as politicians hurried to determine the length of military service, and invented income tax.

At that time, events were coming thick and fast, leaving no time to catch one's breath. In the press, a daily jamboree of headlines and sport items began to supplant comment and opinion, where each day brought only a renewed desire to put the clock back.

At that time the French people thought they were going through a bad patch. There were more earthquakes around Aix-en-Provence than ever before. The Seine burst its banks, flooding the streets of Paris, transforming the Île St-Louis into a lakeside village and making a new landmark of the *Zouave* statue on the Pont d'Alma, up to its goatee in water. An infamous gang of bank-robbers was sowing panic, and the entire police force had to be mobilised before its leader, Bonnot, was arrested. At the same time, though, the people of France thought they were living in remarkable times. A woman, Marie Curie, was elected to a professorship at the Sorbonne and awarded the Nobel Prize. Elsewhere, another woman, Sarah Bernhardt, was taking the theatrical world by storm, in the Paris theatre named in her honour. The cinematograph had its own idol, the actor Max Linder, earning a million francs a year, and its temple, the *Palais Gaumont*, whose 3,400 seats made it the biggest theatre in the world.

It was a time of innovation in the arts. Picasso was painting the *Demoiselles d'Avignon*, Ravel composing *Daphnis et Chloé*, Gide writing *Strait is the Gate*. The flurry of masterpieces did not prevent some slippage, however, and art was also developing its sensationalist side. In Le Figaro, a group of 'intellectuals' published a manifesto proclaiming the roaring motorcar aesthetically superior to the *Winged Victory of Samothrace*.

At that time, dreams of open spaces and adventure were being fulfilled. An American explorer called Peary reached the North Pole, while the Norwegian Amundsen conquered the South. A Frenchman, the aviator Louis Blériot, made the first cross-Channel flight.

At that time, around 1910, it was clear that not everyone would be pleased all of the time. A certain Léon Bloy asserted that sport was 'the surest way to produce a generation of delinquent cretins'.

Nonetheless, in athletics, Jean Bouin was becoming three-time cross-country champion of the world. Aviator Roland Garros held the world altitude record at 5,601 metres. In boxing, Georges Carpentier won the European welterweight title at the age of twenty, followed by the middleweight and heavyweight categories. Lucien Gaudin, a champion with both the foil and the épée, was hailed as a master of fencing. In football, Pierre Chayriguès, with his extraordinary movement and ability, was reinventing goalkeeping. And in rugby, the French national team had their first victory over Scotland in the Five Nations championship.

In tennis, Max Decugis and André Gobert at last ensured that French names would be engraved on the Wimbledon trophy. In cycling, once-lowly road riders gained the status of kings, and their names – Lucien Petit-Breton, Louis Trousselier, Gustave Garrigou, Eugène Christophe – were becoming legend as they rode improbable routes called the *Tourmalet* or the *Galibier*.

It was a time of change for cycling. At first, between 1885 and 1900, it was only the 'speed school' that counted, dubbed the 'sporting aristocracy' by an in-vogue journalist. At the Paris velodromes (of which there were a good half-dozen), officials were decked out in top hats and tails, while the champions sported extravagant nicknames. Perhaps the most celebrated, the American Zimmermann, was nicknamed 'the Flying Yankee'. Speed was an international language. The French, who boasted talented sprinters blessed with larger-than-life personalities – Bourillon sang at the Opera, Jacquelin lived it up in Parisian high-society – were up against English and German riders drawn to the tracks by the prize money. In 1900, the winner of the speed competition known as the 'Grand Prix de l'Exposition' carried off a prize of 15,000 francs: a substantial sum, considering that the total purse for the first Tour de France in 1903 amounted to 20,000 francs.

Compared to these sprint aces, road cyclists were seen as rejects of the velodrome. According to Paul Ruinart, future 'Monsieur V.C.L.' at the Vélo-Club de Levallois and grand old man of the track, the roadsters were admired for their endurance and energy, but alongside the thoroughbred champion sprinters, they looked like second-class racers. 'They lacked style and, it must be said, sartorial elegance.' In those days, a trip to the velodrome had all the atmosphere of a day at the races. Thus, at the Parc des Princes, a certain number of racers known for their fine manners were permitted to make an appearance in their regalia amongst the spectators at the weigh-in, according to a list drawn up by the director himself, Henri Desgrange. Then, suddenly, the speed trials went from chic to sham. There were just too many races, the same old challenges, and too much of the big top about them. To cap it all, the planned introduction of betting (which explained the length of the 666.66m track at the Parc des Princes) was condemned by the authorities. At the same time, and equally suddenly, some extraordinary road races captured the public imagination, stimulated in large measure by the newspapers that often doubled as race organisers.

With the ten-yearly Paris-Brest-Paris race (1891), and the classic annuals Bordeaux–Paris (1891), Paris–Roubaix and Paris–Tours (1896), the Tour de France (1903), Liège-Bastogne-Liège (1894), the Tour of Lombard (1905) and the Milan–San Remo (1907), road racing acquired its great landmark events, which would win the loyalty of its followers. After several false starts, it had established itself, with the support of the bicycle and tyre manafacturers. The sport was rigorously controlled: so rigorously, indeed, that the French Cycling Union came to be known as 'the old tyrant'. Since the creation of the International Cycling Union in 1900, cycling had gone international.

It was free, and it was popular.

One could say that cycling had truly arrived when, in 1907 and 1908, Petit-Breton achieved consecutive wins in the Tour de France.

This is where Octave Lapize comes onto the scene.

* * * * *

For a long time, it was a well-known fact that Octave Lapize was born in Montrouge in 1889. The son of a coal merchant, his was another face in the portrait gallery of those wretched purveyors of coal or beer, hardened by adversity and therefore well equipped to succeed, far from their native Auvergne whose sons it could not sustain.

It's a nice story, but not actually true.

Lapize's first biographer, Charles Ravaud, sowed the first seeds of doubt in his 1912 pamphlet: Octave's father was born not in the Auvergne, but at La Tour-du-Pin in the Isère. Living near the Col de Porte naturally meant that the young Lapize would make an excellent climber.

Still nice, but not true either.

The true story begins elsewhere, genealogically speaking. It is no less nice, but perhaps more surprising. Octave (Louis) Lapize was born on 24 October 1887 at six in the evening, at number 49 Rue Bénard, in Paris's fourteenth *arrondissement*.

Octave (Jules) Lapize, his father, was born on 22 December 1859, in Mende in the Lozère.

César (Émile) Lapize was his grandfather. César, father of Jules (Octave), and grandfather of Louis (Octave), was a merchant of Mende, living on the Rue Impériale in the reign of Emperor Napoleon III. From the illustrious ring of their names and address, we are forced to conclude that the Lapizes of Mende came of decidedly good stock.

They had done so for several generations. The very parchment promoting the Lapizes to high rank is still kept in an attic. It was in 1701, in the time of Louis XIV, when the Lapize family was residing in the Seneschalsy of Gourdon (now the *Sous-Préfecture* of the Lot), that a distant ancestor was distinguished, according to the document in the attic: a decree issued by the province of Languedoc (folio 258) and the city of Toulouse (no. 258).

> *By order issued on this eighteenth day of the month of March in the year 1701, of the Commissioners General of the Council assigned to the matter of coats of arms,*
>
> *Those of Hugues Vidal Lapize, Privy Counsellor to the King in his councils, Lieutenant-General in the Seneschalsy of Gourdon,*
>
> *Such as they are painted and represented here, having been received, have been registered in the General Armoury, in the volume labelled Toulouse, in consequence of the payment of fees set forth by the Tariff and Order of the Council of the twentieth of November of the year 1696, in testimony whereof the present certification has been issued in Paris by us,*

Charles d'Hozier, Privy Councillor, and keeper of the
General Armoury of France. Made in Paris, on the
twenty-fourth day of the month of March in the year
1707.

[signed] d'Hozier

We should not let ourselves be over-awed by this parchment, bearing in mind that coats of arms were routinely obtained in return for generous contributions to the coffers of the realm. We should also note that, although they do not contest the authenticity of the crest, heraldry experts have suggested that it was in fact awarded to one Hughes Vidal, where 'Lapize' refers to a small domain rather than a patronymic. Nonetheless, the fact remains that the parchment came into the family's possession and was handed down as far as the Lapizes of Mende, whose 'heritage' is still something of a mystery.

But let us return to our Lapize in Paris.

His birth certificate, registered at the town hall of the 14th *arrondissement* by Philippe Laziès, Mayor and Registrar, yields some interesting information. In 1887, Octave's father was 27 years old and working as a brewer: a *brasseur.*

The Rue Bénard, where he had his address, was in a district known as Petit-Montrouge. Octave's mother, originally from the Cantal region, was twenty; her profession is recorded as 'wine merchant'. The first witness, a family friend, was a coalman by trade.

The father, Octave Lapize, was the ninth of twelve children, and the only one, apart from an elder sister Mathilde (to whom we will be returning), to escape the seminary and the religious education imposed by the family. Both of them went up to Paris. Here, on the Quai de Jemmapes in the 10th *arrondissement*, Octave the elder delivered beer and brewed a little of his own, naming one of his creations 'Creole' in honour of his wife Pauline's dark locks. His pride and joy was his dray, and he took great care of the wagon and horses, to which he was very attached. The vehicle also brought much happiness to young Octave, who from an early age was allowed to accompany his father's deliveryman on his rounds. Sometimes, at Octave's request, the driver would give the children of the best customers a ride on the wagon. At the Café-Restaurant Peyrot, near the St. Louis Hospital, Octave would insist particularly on picking up the daughter of the house, Juliette.

Octave the younger enjoyed a happy childhood. Cherished as an only son, and doted upon by a mother whose adoration he reciprocated, he was nonetheless an unspoiled child. An excellent student and a fast learner, he was also an unruly boy, and the family still relates how he once swam across the Canal St-Martin to escape a hiding. Leaving school at fourteen, Octave began to work with his father, finding that the physical work suited him down to the ground. We know little about Octave's life between the ages of 15 and 18. We do not know, for instance, who first sat him on a bicycle. Whoever it was, it was not his father, who had no time for such pursuits. He had to cycle in secret, and his mother secretly repaired the trousers that suffered during these clandestine rides. But Octave the elder was no fool, and put up strong resistance to what would become his son's exclusive passion. There were quarrels, we hear, and even the occasional wallop on the backside. But nothing could stop this boy, who dreamed of becoming a racer one day. Through some acquaintances, he came into contact with the French Amateur Cyclists' Federation, and was clandestinely subscribed to the Sporting Union of the 10th *arrondissement*. In the spring of 1905, at the age of 17, he took part in 50-kilometre and 100-kilometre brevets. It was probably for the best that he was unplaced, because his father knew nothing of these escapades.

Octave, however, was toughened up by such resounding failures, which were due largely to rashness and inexperience. He occasionally even embarked upon brevets of 150 kilometres! One day, leaving Pontoise on the climb towards Ennery, he came to a complete standstill, collapsed and fell asleep by the side of the road. Clocking-in time early the next morning was a painful moment for the young man. His father and boss could not permit him to waste his life. He had but one concern, one obsession: to provide his son with an honest trade by which to earn a living and make a decent life for himself. There was no place for bicycles in the rat race, and Octave senior would hear no more about it. Heated discussions ensued between father and son, and difficult times for Pauline. That is, until a certain day in August 1906, at Villiers-sur-Marne.

Where? At the beginning of the twentieth century, Villiers-sur-Marne was a small, rural village of the Seine-et-Oise with around 2,000 citizens. The pride of Villiers was its railway station, on the Paris-Mulhouse line that had opened in 1857. It was a halt in the outer suburbs of Paris, renowned for the frequency of its trains and the modesty of its ticket prices: in 1899, 240,000 passengers passed through Villiers station. On Sundays, day-trippers would arrive in large numbers for the area's reputedly excellent air, and its no less excellent restaurants and dance halls. Moreover, Villiers-sur-Marne, lying to the east of Paris, was the first *commune* outside the Seine *département* and its cordon of red tape. In 1898, the Prefect of the Seine had decreed a speed limit of 12 kph for cars on his territory. Thanks to this decision, it fell to Villiers to be designated the starting-point, on 7 July 1898, for the first international automobile race from Paris to Amsterdam and back. There was considerable public excitement at the send-off, but the finish was met with indifference, except for the French victor, Monsieur Charron, and his Panhard-Levassor, whose genuine success brought in more than 120,000 francs worth of orders.

All very well, you may say, but what has this to do with that famous day in August 1906? Well, I'm coming to that. On Villiers' main thoroughfare, the Rue de Paris, there were no fewer than three cafés on a cycling theme, such as 'Au Rendez-Vous' or 'The Cyclist's Rest', where tourers would stop off for refreshments on their way – and again on the way back. The Café Séminel was held in particularly high esteem: in 1898,

Constant Séminel had created the Villiers Cycling Club, and racers would arrange to meet at his establishment. This café served as the point of departure for races running to Meaux, Compiègne, Château-Thierry and even all the way to Rheims. With his 10th *arrondissement* club turning to the East of Paris, Octave regularly attended these events. He did not take part, however, because his father, who often came to the area, would be sure to find out and fly into a rage.

However, back to 5 August 1906...

On that particular day the Villiers Cycling Club, which was well known in the region, organised its Grand Prix, a 96-kilometre 'classic' from Villiers to Coulommiers and back. The race naturally set off from the Café Seminel, while the finish line was at the Route de la Malnoue, on the edge of Noisy-le-Grand. The race was of a sufficiently high category for the newspaper *L'Auto* to publish a list of the entrants, of which there were 93, and at number 70 – as if hiding at the back of the classroom – was one Octave Lapize (Sporting Union10th).

The 6 August edition of *L'Auto* reveals what happened next.

> Villiers-sur-Marne had not seen a race with so many participants since the start of the Paris–Brussels. The Villiers Cycling Club has scored an undeniable success in the organisation of its interclub meeting, with 84 of 93 entrants picking up their race numbers. At 8:20am a crowd of competitors dashed off in pursuit of victory. Many fewer returned, as such hopes were decimated by punctures and, more particularly, falls. At the turning point in Coulommiers, 60 riders were counted, the leading group of 23 men passing at 9:50am. Of this number, only 37 crossed the line before the officials' departure.
>
> At the finish, on the Route de la Malnoue, there were 11 riders left at the front, and the trial

was won at the posts by Lapize, for whom this
is a first win.

We hope to see more of this young man.

Octave had won in two hours and 59 minutes, at an average
of 32 kph!

Not yet 19, Octave had seen his name in the newspaper
that organised the Paris–Brussels and the Tour de France. The
whole of the cycling world was talking about this overnight
phenomenon, who was also approached by one of the
capital's most celebrated clubs, the Paris Cyclists' Union. And,
miraculously, Octave senior was proud of his son's achievement
for the first time. All the prouder since he had been nursing a
plan to buy a plot of land in Villiers, upon which he envisaged
building the *café-auberge* which would bear his name. And the
address of the café? On the Route de la Malnoue: almost on the
very finishing line crossed for his first victory by Octave Lapize
who, shortly afterwards and for all time, would become 'the
boy from Villiers'.

* * * * *

In 1907, everything changed.

Now 19, Octave knew there was a chance that his dream of
becoming a cycling champion could come true. Little by little,
his father was giving him his head, as long as he worked his
hours in winter, and found a replacement for when he was
away. It was even rumoured that Octave the elder was footing
the bill for a rented cubicle at the municipal track. After all, if
respectable people were falling over each other to tell him what
a talented cyclist his son was, he was not far from admitting

that a good racer could earn his living on a bike. The respectable people in question were the heads of the Paris Cyclists' Union, a distinguished club, highly regarded not just anywhere, but in the capital itself where its headquarters was the *Taverne Zimmer* in the Place du Châtelet. Its president, Dr Raoul Baudot, was also a man of some standing, as a former surgeon at the Hospitals of Paris. Most importantly, his deputy, the vice-president, was one Alphonse Steinès. This Steinès was a key figure (all his life, Octave Lapize would refer to him as 'Mr President'). A high-ranking member of the French Cycling Union (UVF), he was responsible for the delicate problem of cyclists' categories.* He was also a correspondent for *L'Auto* newspaper and for Desgrange, who entrusted him with technical missions on the Tour de France.

With such notables on the scene, everything changed. First of all, Octave began to look like a racer. He wore a fine jersey: his club's blue jersey with a red trim, which the whole of France would come to recognize. From now on, he would belong to the 'real' Federation, the French Cycling Union, which had managed to outmanoeuvre the powerful French Athletic Sports Union (UFSA), the French Cyclists' Union and the Amateur Cycling Federation, to which the young Lapize had belonged in 1906 through his club, the Sporting Union of the 10th *arrondissement*.

One of the main roles of the French Cycling Union (UVF for short) was to organise national championships. 16 March

---

* The problem of categorizing cyclists lasted the whole of the twentieth century. In 1900 there were four categories: the first and second were reserved for track cyclists, and the third and fourth for road racers. The purpose of the fourth professional class was to balance the ranks of the amateurs. This role was later assigned to other categories: independents, and candidates for professional status. The French Cycling Union never ceased to reflect upon this important question. It is a little-known fact that the Union established the single licence system, on 25 November 1920. The International Cycling Union rejected this initiative, much to the chagrin of the French Union's President, Léon Breton. It was not until 1993 that the amateur and professional categories officially disappeared and all competitions became 'open'.

1907 was the day of the French Cyclo-cross Championship, which was open to both amateurs and professionals. And guess what? On the evening of 16 March, the French Cyclo-cross Champion was none other than Octave Lapize! I am not joking, although I should be a bit more precise about the true status of the event. First, it was something of a non-event, and its reverberations did not fill more than a quarter of a column in *L'Auto*. Secondly, it was a type of trial that we would find most surprising today. The newspaper's correspondent notes that 'the course was made up of some quite difficult climbs, sheer drops and paths, unsuitable for cycling, through fields and woods', which would appear to correspond more or less to a modern cyclo-cross event (except that it must have been a nightmare with a fixed wheel), but the journalist adds that the event was over about 25 kilometres of 'a route that was half demarcated and half left to the competitors' initiative.' In other words, this was almost in the realm of orienteering, which makes it easier to understand why the officials gathered at the finish might include a representative from the War Ministry, one Lieutenant Testard.

Nonetheless, Octave was the genuine champion of an authentic French championship. The race unfolded in front of quite a throng of sports enthusiasts, who noted that it had been a long time since the Mont Valérien had seen such a crowd. 58 participants set off along slippery tracks, waterlogged from the previous night's downpour. The race report, on the other hand, was rather dry: 'We recorded victory for Lapize of the PCU who covered the distance in 1 hour 43 minutes and 23 seconds, 10 seconds ahead of Pagès.' It is left to the biographer's imagination to fill in with a more flattering commentary. If we compare the winning time with the distance of the race – 1 hour 45 minutes for 25 kilometres – we can conclude that this cross-country race was no stroll in the woods. The last placed rider, number 45, rolled up an hour and 20 minutes later. The event is not to be taken as a joke, nor even lightly, because the championship's fourth place, five minutes off the lead, went to none other than Eugène Christophe, ninth in the Tour de

France the previous year.* This would suggest that the winning rider must have been pretty good.

He was. On the road, Octave performed creditably, even if victory itself was to elude him. It was in the month of June that he really emerged. 9 June was Paris-Chartres or, more precisely, the 'Prix Charles Ducom' organised by the Chartres Vélo-Club. There were 101 riders at the start at 8:30am. At 10:44, a group of seven arrived at the finishing line. Holding fourth place in the line for a long time, Lapize of the PCU came through with a strong sprint to win. Looking closely at the report, we can find this brief but perspicacious comment: 'If this rider, always well placed, was lacking a first big victory, he carried it off yesterday and has good grounds for hoping it will be the first of many.'

I couldn't have put it better myself. On Sunday 23 June, he took second place in Paris-Rouen: only second, but after two punctures. The strange thing is that from the very next day, Octave began training at the Buffalo velodrome – behind motorcycles, with the aim of landing the world amateur championship. There was only one motor-paced event each year for amateurs, and young riders felt they should not miss this opportunity to gain professional status. Lapize did not get anywhere and returned to the road. Good job, too, I am tempted to say.

He came back very strongly. On 30 June, he won the Prix Valor at Brie-Comte-Robert. On 21 July, he was at Villiers-sur-Marne at the start of the Paris-Reims, a race open to professionals. He came fourth, behind Brocco and Cruchon, about whom we will speak again later, and Trousselier, already much talked-about thanks to his Tour de France win in 1905. One week later, in the Paris championship between Versailles and Orléans, he was beaten again by Cruchon and Brocco. Lapize could only manage seventh place, due to the fact that he suffered a 'violent

---

* Eugène Christophe (1885-1970), an exemplary rider and a man of great merit, was a professional cyclist from 1904 to 1924. Outside his brilliant road racing career, he was 12-time French cyclo-cross champion.

collision with a policeman during the sprint.' In August, he was one of a 10-strong French delegation taking part in the renowned Tour of Belgium. This was a well-planned race with six stages, all under 100 kilometres, and against powerful Belgian opposition. On the third day, he won at Anvers 'in front of a thousand spectators outside the velodrome and three thousand inside.' He returned from Belgium in good shape, and just at the right moment.

On 8 September, the UVF held the French road cycling championship at Nancy. And what do you think? By the evening of 8 September, Octave Lapize was French amateur road racing champion. This really did set people talking... (two days later, Octave's photograph made it in *L'Auto* for the first time).

The *parcours* for this 100-kilometre race was an out-and-back route between Nancy and Châtel-Nomeny. For the 23 who started, the weather was perfect. The first part was animated by the impetuous Brocco, who led for a long time, and was only caught on the return leg. At the finish, Lapize broke away cleanly from the bunch. A lad from Amiens, Wirtz, took second place, and the Parisian rivals Brocco and Cruchon third and fourth respectively. The papers did not fail to mention Lapize's victories for his first real year, beginning with his cyclo-cross title. *L'Auto*, the best informed, reported: 'Almost unheard of last year, Octave Lapize is one of those plucky unknowns who make these races such a success... Just recently, in the Tour of Belgium, he took one of the six stages, no mean feat considering the difficulties the French riders had to overcome. To this glittering crown has just been added the finest jewel an amateur can covet... Octave Lapize is not only a champion, but also an honest and loyal rider, and a good comrade to his PCU team-mates. At an extraordinary meeting last night, the Committee of the PCU decided to present a champion's gold cross to the new holder of the tricolour jersey.'

So ended the year, crowned with gold. I mean that Octave did not have to settle for the usual prizes in kind (bicycles, tyres, tubes and other medals) that were given out to the winners of amateur races. Although his name was not cited, Cycles Labor, 'the rigid machine that rolls like a dream', took out a quarter-page newspaper advertisement the day after a 'triumph in the 50-kilometre race at La Cipale.' This anonymous triumph had gone to Lapize. Perhaps we can assume that he received some sort of reward. But there was a very good reason for the omission of his name: the UVF was leading a crusade to defend amateur status. Some of its members even thought of creating a Pure Championship that might help purge the peloton of thugs. Was the UVF over-reacting? Alas, no. In the middle of August, at its headquarters on the Boulevard des Italiens, three masked riders had beaten up its staff in an operation likened to a 'hold-up'. There really were some hooligans in the peloton.

At the beginning of 1908, the man wearing the French amateur champion's tricolour jersey was certainly no thug. They taught good manners at the Paris Cyclists' Union. Octave Lapize at 20 was considered a 'modest and pleasant' young man. These are the words of its president Alphonse Steinès, but the opinion was shared by all observers. Amongst these, the young manager Paul Ruinart, soon to be recognized as a master at spotting champions, predicted that 'Octave Lapize will be the best rider of his generation, because he has all the gifts of the perfect cyclist.' It could have gone to Octave's head, but he began the season modestly. His main rivals, Brocco and Cruchon, had turned professional, but Lapize still lived by the rhythms of the PCU, taking part in the excursions and military brevets organised by his club. On 12 April, he came second in a 100-kilometre brevet that was won by Eugène Christophe.

Given his amateur status, let us dwell for a moment on the most glorious of sporting events: the Olympic Games, for which Octave was selected. In 1908, because Rome had pulled out at the last minute, the Games were to be hosted by London. Officially, they were to last for six months, from 20 April to 30 October. However, the main competitions were scheduled for July. They went almost unnoticed in France, the press offering tiny coverage.

After all, it was the middle of the Tour de France!

A hastily-constructed Olympic stadium housed almost all the events. Around the central pitch, an athletics track of 535.45m (being in England, it had to be a third of a mile). This was bordered in turn by a cycling track running to 666m (God save our Metric System!). Inside, on the edge of the pitch, a 100m x 17m pool had been excavated for the swimming events. The English had planned on a grand scale, building enough stands and terraces to hold 70,000 spectators. So much for the statistics.

Remarkably, the one thing the English had not foreseen was the weather.

Monday 13 July, the day of the opening ceremony, was a washout, and the stands were empty. It was still raining on Tuesday 14th and Wednesday 15th and the organisers dropped the entrance charge to entice spectators in. The British judges' bad faith added to the general gloom. A outraged American official declared that the jury had 'planted the last nail in the coffin of English fair-play.' It was still wet on 16 July, when the cyclists entered the lists. This was unfortunate, because the wooden track was slippery, causing many falls. In the sprint event, the Frenchman Maurice Schilles, a clear winner, was scandalously disqualified by the judges. In the 100-kilometre race – which took place, mark you, on the track and not the road – Octave Lapize came in third behind two unsporting Englishmen who had given him a hard time. But Lapize did not protest. The French officials were tired of complaining. L'Auto, on the same day, was completely wrapped up in François Faber's victory in the Metz-Belfort stage of the Tour de France.

Oh, yes, the Tour de France. Believe it or not, it was not until two years later, at the finish of the first Paris–Roubaix stage of the 1910 Tour, that Lapize told the story of his Olympics. On that day, he had come in for some rough treatment from the Belgian Vanhouwaert, and had to settle for third place. It all came back to him then, and he told the story calmly:

For a moment, I thought I was back in London during the 100 kilometres on the track. Bartlett and his minions had boxed me in so much that I ended up in third place, like today. I had hoped for something better... Then again, even if I was robbed, I wasn't the worst off. Schilles should have had his title, but was disqualified on a very dubious technicality.

The press was amazed to hear that Lapize had been at the Olympics. As if to try to excuse their ignorance, they risked one last question: 'And the Baron de Coubertin?' Octave, who had a good memory, replied: 'I know he was there, but I didn't see him. Personally, I met the Duchess of Westminster who presented me with the bronze medal, while Queen Alexandra awarded the gold and silver to Bartlett and Denny.' Two names which would never trouble the cycling historian again.

Back to France in 1908. On 26 July, in the Paris Championship held at Saint-Germain, observers were surprised to see Octave defeated in the sprint by a certain Marcault: by the smallest margin, but beaten all the same. After the finish it emerged that, following an accident, he had completed the race on a borrowed bicycle. It must be said that 1908 was not a fortunate year for Lapize, but victory eventually smiled on him once again on 2 August in the Paris-Auxerre, a race officially recognized as 'first category'. Octave won that day after covering the 150 kilometres in four hours and 47 minutes, at an average of over 31 kph. The 5 August edition of *L'Auto* carried a quarter-page advertisement trumpeting that 'The 150-kilometre Paris-Auxerre was won by Lapize, on a Labor cycle fitted with Hutchinson-Monofil tyres.'

Although it featured an amateur rider, this advertisement must have been allowed because it was classed as a first-category race. A case of class war, perhaps.

On 14 August, Octave was not happy at the finish of the Paris-Dieppe. He was classed second, 10 centimetres behind the winner, Sabatier. Third-placed Bonnet tried to involve Octave in challenging this decision. But that was not Octave's style. Then came the French championships, where he was naturally the favourite. The race was over the traditional distance of 100 kilometres, this time from Amiens to Beauvais and back. Thirteen riders broke away, but there were only 12 at the finish, because 'Lapize punctured and the rest bolted,' according to a *débutant* named Henri Pélissier, who came in sixth. Octave was 13th, then, while the new French champion was Paul Mazan, the brother of Petit-Breton, who had just won the Tour de France and whose real name was Lucien Mazan.

Was Octave disappointed by this run of bad luck on the road? Or did it lead him to believe that his ticket to professional status would be found on the track? After all, it had been by coming third in the world amateur motor-paced racing championship that Brocco had won recognition and employment. In any case, on 6 September, Octave Lapize was at the starting post of the municipal track in Vincennes, in the line-up for the Bol d'Or, modelled on the professional race but contested over six hours instead of twenty-four.

For the first hour, which was not paced, he was an observer. He took the lead during the second hour, as soon as the motorcycles came onto the track. Paul Mazan abandoned the race in the third hour, while Lapize just carried on in his own sweet way to victory, having covered 226 kilometres in the six hours. The runner-up was two and a half kilometres behind. This was a huge success, and Lapize would stick to the track from then on.

Those in the know were aware that he was training behind motorcycles, and on 19 September at the Parc des Princes… but I'm going too fast myself.

19 September was a Saturday and there was great excitement at the Parc des Princes, because the finest meeting of the year, the Grand Prix de la République, was scheduled for the next day. The nine best sprinters in the world had been invited. Amongst the crowd that had gathered at the trackside, was a journalist from *L'Auto*, who wrote:

Taking advantage of the ideal, if slightly chilly, conditions, the PCU's Octave Lapize launched his bid for a new hour record behind motorcycles a little before 5am. The timekeeper was our good friend Monsieur de Perrodil. Never was a record broken with such ease. Lapize was grinning from start to finish, and there is little doubt that, with better advice, he could have added an extra kilometre.

With a smile on his lips, Octave Lapize became world record-holder, posting a most regular schedule:

10 kilometres	7'42.0"
20 kilometres	14'50.6"
30 kilometres	21'54.6"
40 kilometres	29'09.2"
50 kilometres	36'30.4"
60 kilometres	43'46.8"
70 kilometres	50'48.2"
80 kilometres	58'00.6"

...and covering a distance of 82.758 kilometres in the hour. The previous record was smashed, improved by 5 kilometres. The International Cycling Union, only recognizing one kind of record, gave the time 'unofficial' status. *L'Auto* reported that the new record holder (his name is not even mentioned at this point!) had ridden a Labor bicycle with Hutchinson tyres, and launched into fulsome praise that reads like a job application: 'In the opinion of all present, Lapize, after only about 15 training sessions, is looking a dangerous threat to the professionals.'

Here was the first testimonial, but there was more to come. 'This young man of twenty summers will be spared the fate of military service, having been declared ineligible. This will doubtless allow him to continue a career that has begun so promisingly.' This was a second invitation to the professional teams' recruiters, but the journalist rounds off his classified ad on a high note, the cherry on the cake: 'He doesn't smoke, he doesn't drink and – an important detail – everyone likes him.' With such a reference, it would be a wonder if Octave did not gain entry to the professional level. Every young rider dreamt of this miraculous ticket to the promised land, as Henri Desgrange makes clear in his paper:

> It is the time of year when all champions in the making, whose only flaw is to be impecunious, strive to find ways to publicize their wares and to arrive at that moment of bliss when a fine racing cycle appears between their legs without costing a thing, the velodrome subscription is paid by the firm, together with a cubicle at the same track and even, perhaps, a salary.

Octave, one suspects, already had the fine racing bicycle safely between his thighs, courtesy of Labor. Such a machine was worth 250 francs, a tidy sum if you consider that this was half the annual salary of a working man. But in order to fulfil his ambitions, the budding champion aimed to do better still: why not 85 kilometres in an hour? He decided to try to break his own record on 24 September, but the attempt was cut short. A report tells us that, 'The amateur Lapize was unable to carry out his attempt at a new hour record, for two equally good reasons: (1) the conditions were against him, and (2) Lapize had forgotten that the telephone was not working, and could not contact the timekeeper.'

At the very least, this information tells us that on 25 September 1908, Octave Lapize was still an amateur in every sense of the word. The evidence is all the more important, because we know that on 17 October Octave Lapize was a professional racing cyclist. It was a fine day for the season's closing gala at the Parc des Princes. At the top of the bill was first a speed contest between the Frenchman Friol, the 1907 world champion, and Denmark's 1908 world champion Ellegaard, and then a middle-distance race (100 kilometres behind motorcycles) involving Ryser of Switzerland, the reigning world champion, the Frenchmen Darragon – twice world champion – and Contenet, the American Nat Butler, a star in his own right, the Englishman Wills, a rider of great promise, and the former amateur champion Octave Lapize. You could imagine a less fiery baptism. This was no fun day out for Octave. The American was in storming form, toying with his opponents and the track record. He dropped Ryser after two and a half laps, Contentet a little further on, and saw off a disgusted Darragon, who abandoned the race. In all the upheaval, Octave came in fourth at 16 laps. Wills was last, although commentators thought he had confirmed his promising beginnings. From this, we can deduce that Lapize's performance was nothing to be ashamed of, and that he had passed his entry exam. Nonetheless, it is surprising to note that in order to become a professional, Lapize, like many other riders, had had to graduate by racing behind heavy motorcycles. In 1908, this was quite a normal move which confounded no-one, except perhaps the 'pink'un': *L'Écho des sports*, the rival paper to *L'Auto* (which was printed on yellow paper).

L'Écho's comments were less than rosy:

> Lapize turned pro in the Autumn. But whatever for, for heaven's sake? To play the clown behind a motorbike! And what a motorbike! If fate had also placed him behind a capable trainer, he might have been able to show us his qualities which, it must be said – and written – are quite brilliant.

This was just the start.

ALL IN ONE GO

Having donated his prizes for the 1908 season to his club – as was the custom at the PCU – Octave Lapize leapt into the deep end at the beginning of 1909. His dive did not make much of a splash because he had not held the attention of the big teams like Alcyon, Peugeot, La Française or even Le Globe. He had been taken on by Biguet, a small manufacturer, whose premises were on the Boulevard Pereire in Paris. This Biguet was an enthusiast and gave his support to less well-known riders, like those, for example, who entered the Tour de France in the independent *'isolé'* category. This less-than-glorious appointment failed to put Octave Lapize senior's mind at rest. He was still sceptical about his son's chances of making a living on a bicycle. If he had known that the Alcyon management had just doubled its competitive edge by taking on Baugé alongside Calais, he would not have been reassured. Moreover, it was a harsh winter, which seemed to go on for ever. On 14 March, it was still snowing in and around Paris.

Either worried or impatient, or both, Octave spread himself too thinly, training and racing indiscriminately, according to some. Others assert that he kept to a regular rhythm of 100-kilometre rides. He took part in cyclo-cross meetings, most notably in the French championship. On the Mont Valérien on Sunday 28 March, the weather was so terrible – the snow had not yet entirely melted – that only 16 riders lined up at the start. Eugène Christophe took the title, and Lapize third place, but he had broken a pedal five kilometres from the finish. This time there was an explanation, but people were taken aback a week later when he abandoned the renowned Coupe Valor. It turned out that he had taken part in and won a 50-kilometre trial that very same morning! It all looked disorganised and rather amateurish. Neither the guiding hand of Biguet, nor the support of a team was anywhere to be seen. It was worrying, because at the same time *L'Auto* was publishing a veritable three-part serial on the Alcyon armada's reconnaissance mission along the route of the Paris–Roubaix, with Faber at its head. More discreetly, but stubbornly, Octave rode alone until the day he bumped into Eugène Christophe in Beauvais, *en route* for Roubaix like himself. Christophe, who, at 24, was only three years older than Lapize, was already an experienced rider and had ridden Paris–Roubaix in 1904. All the same, he was scarcely better off than his young companion, having just completed his two years of military service. Christophe had the heart of an elder brother, and the novice Lapize was happy to ride alongside him as far as Doullens. The young man naturally asked for any pointers concerning the route, but also wondered what placing he could hope to achieve in such a major race. Without a moment's hesitation, his companion replied that, barring accidents, he should finish in the top five. Stunned at first, then reassured, Octave went so far as to let him into a secret: if he was not among the first 10 riders, his father was going to make him come back to work immediately. A job had been found, and the contract was ready to be signed. In case of failure, Octave Lapize would be a coal deliveryman at Jackson's on the Quai de la Loire. No need to look far: Quai de la Loire was an extension of the Quai de Jemmapes. Octave senior was being as obliging as ever.

With fear in his belly, Octave the younger strove to perfect his form by the time of the big day: Paris–Roubaix on Sunday 11 April. The press spoke of nothing else. Charles Ravaud, the pre-eminent writer on *L'Auto*, announced a record, even before he started weighing up the favourites' chances: the number of entrants was the highest ever, at 132. After selecting a shortlist of 20 or so names amongst whom the victor must necessarily figure, Ravaud, in his lordly fashion, adds a small postscript:

'Of the outsiders, Lapize, Duboc and Léonard might have the opportunity to prove themselves outstanding roadsters once and for all. But we will have to sacrifice them with regret, their past form being too inconclusive for an event of this stature.'

* * * * *

So, what was the Paris–Roubaix like in those days? By 1909, its 14th year, the race was already a classic. Since the organiser was *L'Auto*, we need only consult the paper (which came out every day, including Sunday) to learn everything about its organisation. This is how *L'Auto*'s reporters stylishly describe the build-up to the race in all its detail, thanks to their dual role as race officials.

Let's just follow them.*

> It is midnight and the last train has just arrived at Chatou, discharging onto the platform a multitude of sports enthusiasts who would not miss the start of the Paris–Roubaix for the world. Along the road, the pinpricks of multi-coloured Chinese lanterns are beginning to puncture the darkness and the files of cyclists are already starting to form. The control point, which will shortly be set up at Bouché's at 47 route de Saint-Germain, is already being invaded by bands of joyful fans killing time by playing cards or singing popular ditties. In a short while they will be saddling up and setting off to take up their vantage points at a good spot 50 kilometres down the road: a climb, perhaps, or a fast descent, depending on the individual taste. As time goes by, the crowd grows both indoors and out, and 'old father Bouché' has to

---

* Our guide here is the journalist Francis Mercier.

intervene to get the traffic moving again. The card games finish and the officials prepare to receive the riders. The first rays of dawn show on the horizon. The grandstand is erected and the president has the list of riders in front of him. His assistant hands out the race numbers that will allow us to recognize the contestants later on. The UVF representative rolls his eyes each time a rider does not have his licence immediately to hand. Five o'clock! The riders arrive, still bleary-eyed, having slept in Chatou. The cold air quickly revives them. The teams are presented, each with its gaggle of admirers.

The signatures are quite intriguing. While some leave a spidery scrawl, betraying their anxiety, others sign calmly and deliberately. These riders, including Faber, Georget, Trousselier, Alavoine have no stage fright. The hour approacheth. Latecomers – there are always some – hastily collect their numbers and hurry to the start, where a good number of contestants are waiting. The officials' cars are prepared, *L'Auto* flags fitted to their bonnets to distinguish them at the control points and on the road. The photographers aim their cameras left and right. It's time! The moment has arrived! Time for a final roll call, and the road is cleared. One last announcement: 'Attention… partez!' and the peloton is off at a cracking pace, quickly followed by an unbelievable mass of pedallers who will chase them as far as the climb at Le Pecq, at six kilometres.

From Le Pecq onwards it was clear that Sunday 11 April 1909 was going to be a glorious day. This Paris–Roubaix was not going to be a race against rain, wind, hail and mud like the year before. The weather was fine and in fact the followers would be surprised – frightened even – by dense storms of swirling black dust the length of the route, which would leave 'the riders looking like coalminers'.

Where in all this was Octave Lapize? What was he up to? In Chatou he had appeared quietly confident. Just for a laugh he had stuck a little paper pig he had found lying around onto his bottle bag (two bottles or flasks of the rider's preferred drink were wedged into a leather bag which was firmly fixed to the handlebars). For the first time, he had to tackle a distance of 276 kilometres in the middle of a peloton swarming with crack riders. Alcyon fielded the largest team, boasting the outgoing winner, the Belgian Vanhouwaert. It was also the best-supported team, with both a manager, Calais, and a *directeur sportif*, Baugé. They also had trainers (on motorcycles), as permitted by the regulations, as far as Beauvais. The Peugeot team had been invited to stay at home, due to a serious disagreement between Messieurs Robert Peugeot and Henri Desgrange. However, the best riders in the stable – the Georget brothers, Passerieu and others – were allowed to race as individuals (the previous Sunday, Émile Georget had been runner-up in Milan–San Remo).

Octave Lapize was not riding as an individual, but he might as well have been.

The Biguet team fielded a grand total of two riders, Lapize and a certain Saillot, who could at least pride himself on a second place in Paris–Tours. Monsieur Biguet was the team's director, manager and *directeur sportif* rolled into one. He did not have the means, of course, to provide Lapize with trainers: a good job, because Lapize thought trainers more of a hindrance than a help, and that they exacerbated the risk of a fall. He decided quite simply to follow the pace set by the Alcyon team, who happened to be the best trainers in the world: with names like Faber, Garrigou and Trousselier.

Passing the climb at Ennery, of which he had such painful memories, Octave found himself with good legs. A little further on at Breteuil, he had an equally good appetite, grabbing some cutlets at the feeding station. These wretched stations, by the way, were his big worry. At Beauvais, there were still 60 riders in the peloton, making signing in at the station somewhat chaotic.

At Amiens, the leaders' group had shrunk by half. Lapize was no longer among them. A puncture had left him two minutes behind the leaders. It is this banal incident (in an era when punctures were part and parcel of the race) that created the spark. A fascinated observer tells the story of his exploit:

> Repairing quickly, Lapize set off again like a man possessed, on a lone charge, head down into the wind. He caught and passed Wattelier, Beaugendre, Cornet, Garrigou and Faber in turn and, in spite of their desperate efforts, none was able to stick to his wheel for more than 50 metres.

After a 22-kilometre chase, he resumed his place among the leaders. But the party was not over. He had not come back at the best point, and he knew it. The place was called Doullens, and the climb there already had its reputation, which would last half a century, as arbiter of the outcome. Twelve riders hit the climb together. At the top, there were only three left at the front: the Belgians Messelis and Vanhouwaert, and a Frenchman, Trousselier. In fact, these three counted as one since they all belonged to the Alcyon fleet.

But Lapize, a few metres behind, with Passerieu on his wheel, gritted his teeth and immediately closed the gap.

Among the five leaders at Arras, Octave began to believe Christophe's prediction. And then there were four, Passerieu dropping out after a fall. For the observers, the race was over: there was no hope for Biguet's new boy, on his own among three experienced Alcyon riders; there was just time to head for the Parc Barbieux for the finish. Anyway, they couldn't see much here, in all the dust. Fifteen kilometres from Roubaix, Vanhouwaert punctured and was unable to rejoin his comrades: now there were just three left to fight it out in the sprint, over six laps of the 400-metre concrete track. But then it became more complicated at the end of the first lap, when Vanhouwaert suddenly reappeared between Trousselier, Messelier and Lapize. On the final lap, Trousselier, after taking the lead, began to show signs of fatigue, even swerving off onto the cinder running track. Lapize, who had sensibly stayed on the outside, swallowed Trousselier unopposed, and Messelis was left to take third place.

The prestigious scoreboard showed Vanhouwaert in fourth and Faber in fifth place.

At the finish, the crowd wavered. Then, disappointment at the defeat of the fast and popular 'Trou-Trou' very quickly turned into admiration at the revelation of 'a young man of great distinction' (he was now 21).

Everyone wanted to hear what the victor had to say. Octave Lapize calmly explained that it had been a fortunate race for him, even though he had had a bit of trouble coming back after his puncture. Then he gave way to his delight: 'Don't ask me for any more details; it's still too fresh for me, as you can see. I've won. I'm out of my mind with joy. It's the best day of my life! But, good God, what a dust storm, and what a crowd!' Indeed, 20,000 spectators gave him an ovation as the *Marseillaise* rang out.

In nine hours, three minutes and 30 seconds, Octave Lapize's life had been turned on its head. In Paris, the staff of *L'Auto*, besieged by requests to know the outcome of the race, had to reply from five in the afternoon to more than 1,000 people by telegraph and telephone alike. One of those impatient to find out was Lucien Petit-Breton, winner of the last Tour de France, who had missed the race through injury.

The following day, Charles Ravaud stated that Lapize was 'a young man whose past matches his future,' apparently forgetting his article of two days before. The headline of *L'Auto* said it all, announcing not just 'a rising star' but, 'The Star is Risen'.

It's a nuance that was not lost on Octave Lapize the elder, who, on learning that his son had won the first prize of 1,000 francs, calculated that the sum represented 20 times the annual salary of a workman. That, presumably, was the moment that

Jackson & Co of Quai de la Loire lost the best worker it never had.

And the moment has come for us to get to know our new champion.

First portrait

I have in front of me a photograph of Octave aged 17. This picture, commissioned from a photographer's studio on the Avenue de la République, nicely illustrates the fact that the Lapizes were a typical *petit-bourgeois* family, keen to send its offspring to a specialist in children's portraits.

Young and handsome with his curly, black hair, elegantly dressed in a three-piece suit, he cuts a fine figure in front of the camera. What strikes me, looking at this photo, even if it was posed or affected, is the young man's innate stylishness, his natural ease.

Four years later, at the age of 21, the light down had flourished into a proud moustache, the teenager into a man. Octave was now Lapize. He had lost none of his elegance, but had grown in strength, if *L'Auto* is to be believed:

> I have in front of me a photograph of Lapize, winner of our 14th Paris–Roubaix. He really has the fine looks of a road rider: the vigorous expression, firm set of the jaw, a steely look, a pointed moustache as befits a racer obliged, during long, tedious hours on the road, to blow kisses to pretty girls. He has a broad chest, well-formed legs, powerful thighs and a grip that no handlebars in the world can withstand when he pulls on a climb.

At the same time, another reporter was more interested in the character than the physique of the man of the moment:

> The winner of Paris–Roubaix scorns public opinion, only listening to his own conscience and to his father,

whose word is law. His 'good-boy-ism' is such that we fear to see him surrounded by a gang of outsiders who will not take very long to relieve him of all the advantages that winning an event like the great Easter Race can bring. Does he have any flaws? Yes, he does, and a big one for a sportsman. He lacks perseverance... He doesn't know how to train, and tires himself out more than anything else; not realizing that the body needs rest, he ends up over-training. Lapize does not drink or smoke. We are told that all his friends are men. Some claim to know about a girl friend, but do not believe them.

This article, published in *L'Écho des sports*, which goes in for humour if not satire, ends on a clumsy note if it is unintentional, but an improper one if it is to be taken at face value: 'On the road, Lapize strains like a deaf man.' On that same day, the afore-mentioned Alphonse Steinès revealed this 'distinguishing feature' when speaking about his protégé: at his military service review panel, Lapize had been discharged due to deafness! (Reliable testimonies from family members report that in an attempt to extract an insect that had flown into his ear, a clumsy examination had caused irreversible damage.) Never before or afterwards did Octave Lapize speak about this invisible disability.

So let's not dwell on it, either.*

---

* In the late 1940s, a close acquaintance of Octave Lapize the elder offered a different version of the champion's deafness in an interview with a local Villiers-sur-Marne journalist: that it was on the recommendation – or rather the insistence – of Octave Lapize's club (the Paris Cyclists' Union) that Octave feigned deafness at the conscription panel's medical, in order to avoid military service.

There are at least two reasons to treat this version with some scepticism: first, it is hard to imagine the rigid father Lapize standing for such conduct in his son and, secondly, it seems improbable that the allegation could have gone unmentioned by all Lapize's contemporaries and commentators, particularly given the amount of jealousy inspired by his repeated successes.

Charles Ravaud, who, as we have seen, was the lead writer at *L'Auto*, refrains from mentioning it in his hagiography. Incidentally, this book, *Octave Lapize*, was ordered and circulated by the cycle and tyre manufacturers that equipped the rider.

> His modest height of 1.65 metres (5ft.5ins) accentuates his remarkably athletic build. Octave Lapize has a well-developed thorax which must measure a good 96 or 97cm. His legs are straight, his arms sufficiently well-muscled to maintain long pressure on the handlebars. His waist is supple and powerful; the upper body moves easily above the pelvis, thanks to a suppleness equalled only in his legs. All in all, Lapize was born to be an acrobat of the strongest sort on the bicycle and in fact he distinguishes himself from many of his comrades by his consummate skill. But however attractive his physique, it does not equal his pyschological strength: Lapize's greatest asset is his confidence, which is the source of his power. And the extraordinary thing about this little man is the merciless way he makes that confidence work for him. Even when you know he is in the peloton, it takes a long time to pick him out. Lapize is to be found wherever there is no flint, wherever there is no wind, wherever there is enough shelter to reduce effort to an absolute minimum. He makes no mistakes, he is able to conserve his strength admirably and to use it when and where necessary. He is a man of impeccable manners, exquisite politeness and admirable modesty.

It is hardly necessary to mention this last quality. Alphonse Steinès never tired of repeating that Lapize – 'Tatave' to his close friends – was a modest and pleasant young man!

I am able to offer one or two alterations to these two descriptions. I have been told in confidence by a source within the family that there was one character trait that the young Octave entirely shared with his father, and which they described (behind their backs) as 'pig-headedness'. He was his father's son. I have also learned that, though far from being gloomy, the young Octave was nonetheless taciturn and something of a stay-at-home. Perhaps because of that damned ear. At 22 years old, he was still living with his parents in Villiers-sur-Marne.

The day after Paris–Roubaix, Octave Lapize embarked upon a new life. In the newspapers he discovered enormous advertisements extolling the merits of Biguet bicycles and, even more so, Dunlop tyres, and realized at the same time that each of these firms was going to pay him a sum equal to the first prize he had won. (It is worth pointing out that at this time, advertising was restricted to posters and the press; there were no brand names on the riders' jerseys.) Here he was suddenly with a 3,000 franc fortune in his pockets, equivalent to the yearly salary of a primary teacher. As he was not indifferent to money, life was looking pretty rosy for Octave.

* * * * *

Two people feeling less in the pink were Calais and Baugé, respectively manager and *directeur sportif* of Alcyon. The very next day after Paris–Roubaix, they were summoned to headquarters at 32 Avenue de la Grande Armée, by their big boss, Monsieur Edmond Gentil. If you will excuse the pun, it was well known in the trade that M. Gentil was no 'Mr Nice Guy'. His employees were asked to pay full attention as he fired off two questions. First of all, how on earth could six of their riders finish in the top seven and yet miss first place, and how could Trousselier, Messelis and Vanhouwaert allow a lone rider to slip past them? Secondly, why was this Octave Lapize fellow, with his brilliant amateur record, not riding for Alcyon?

Calais and Baugé were ordered to remedy this double affront by engaging the services of the new phenomenon. 'Good Old Biguet' was duly approached, wooed and, truth to tell, leaned on fairly heavily. Perhaps he would consider letting dear Octave go, in return for a substantial fee? But Biguet stood firm, taking pride in showing the world that he could manufacture 'the perfect machine', as his workshops proclaimed.

Octave Lapize, as far as we can tell, was not approached directly. He was extremely busy. He had quickly understood that he could take immediate advantage of his victory by taking up a series of contracts on the track. He had proved his worth 'in every branch of cycling,' and from winning a race behind heavy motorcycles at the Parc des Princes, he proceeded to a 100-kilometre tandem-paced event at Buffalo. He was free to choose his own races – 'Good Old Biguet' lacked the means to race abroad or to engage in such a heavy financial undertaking as the Bordeaux–Paris – and Octave did not return to the road until 9 May, for the French Championship. Alcyon, with a score to settle, and Peugeot (with whom Desgrange was by now seeing eye to eye) laid down the law, but Lapize on his Biguet confirmed his true worth by coming a respectable fourth.

It was not until six weeks later that he was again to be found at the start of a classic. At 1am on 20 June, he was among 55 starters in the Paris–Brussels, a 406-kilometre event. During the night, 15 or so riders broke away and didn't hang about, covering the 130 kilometres to Épernay in four hours. It was a fast pace, then, but as he was leaving Épernay Lapize found himself at the edge of the road. The repair must have been as much of a mess as the commentary itself because, according to *L'Auto*, 'He repaired rapidly, but lost five minutes.' All eyes were on the young man, to see if he would repeat his Paris–Roubaix performance. Observers noted that he made a brave effort, valiantly keeping up a terrific pace to catch the leaders, and clawing back two minutes over 15 kilometres. But, crossing Reims, he broke his saddle. 'Then,' writes a witness, 'he was overcome by despair, and abandoned the race.'

The misfortune was quickly forgotten because the Tour de France was already looming. Good Old Biguet broke open the piggy bank, recruiting three new riders to form a five-man team in accordance with that year's rules. Lapize and Saillot were joined by reinforcements in the shape of a Swiss rider, Leclerc, a Belgian, Defraye, and a Frenchman, Cruchon, an old acquaintance of Octave's. Talking of Cruchon, the observers pointed out sharply that he had ridden Paris–Brussels for Alcyon, but here he was riding for Biguet a week later. Immediatey there were mutterings that this Cruchon might well mark his début with a far more important transaction. A few quid pro quo, perhaps. People would have to wait and see, however, because the time of reckoning was some way off. On 5 July, one year after his London Olympics, Octave Lapize hurled himself into the Tour de France. There were 147 entrants, including – for the first time – the Italians, with Ganna at their head. The first stage, from Paris to Roubaix, favoured Lapize, who slipped deftly into the successful breakaway of 12 riders who battled it out for victory in the sprint.

This time, in Roubaix, Alcyon's Vanhouwaert and Faber finished ahead of Lapize, who came in a happy third. A rest day followed, during which the weather deteriorated.* By the start of the Roubaix-Metz stage, it had become absolutely dreadful. François Faber, who relished cold and wet conditions, began his spree (he would win five successive stages). He rode into Metz alone, half an hour ahead of Lapize, who also arrived on his own for second place in the stage and in the general classification. The Biguet team could hardly believe their success, until they learned how much their in-house champion had suffered. Sand, thrown up by his rear wheel, had got between his shorts and his skin: 'His flesh was red-raw.' For the 300 kilometres from Metz to Belfort, the same abominable weather persisted and Faber left the rest far behind. Even Christophe, a tough rider, stood third, at one hour. Of Lapize, the only news over the wires was that he had passed Nancy very late. The next day, it was confirmed that he had again suffered terribly. In Nancy, he had

---

* From the first Tour in 1903 until its 18th edition in 1924, each stage (which, incidentally, was very long) was followed by a rest day. This arrangement allowed those arriving late, often by several hours, to gain the minimum of rest they needed to be able to continue the race.

bought a pair of trousers to make himself more comfortable and, above all, had found a doctor to inject him with cocaine to dull the pain. Then he had turned his handlebars over and, like a tourist, finally rolled halfheartedly into Belfort at nightfall. Nonetheless, he started both Belfort-Lyon and the fifth stage from Lyon to Grenoble. In Annecy, after 195 of the stage's 311 kilometres, Lapize's forks broke. It was all over. He threw in the towel. The race followers saluted his courage.

He returned to Villiers disappointed but unbroken. Full of admiration for the irresistible Faber (who won the Tour, of course), Lapize had come to the conclusion that he could recuperate quite quickly, and that stage races should suit him well. This was still the conviction of Monsieur Gentil, who returned to the attack and finally made his colleague Biguet agree to let him have Octave Lapize. Lapize to Alcyon was the transfer of the year, and he was about to mark his début in style.

The first installment came with the decision of Lapize's new firm to enter Milan-Varese. On his first appearance in Italy, Octave would be covered in glory by winning the event, a proper 246-kilometre race, ahead of Ganna, a real champion who had taken the Giro and Milan–San Remo. It was Tuesday 12 September.*

Episode Two in Lapize's move to Alcyon, this time a mock-heroic one, took place on 27 September. On that Monday in 1909, the papers announced Octave Lapize's victory in Paris–Tours. A first win on his first race in France for Alcyon! The only

---

* Octave Lapize's victory in the Milan-Varese calls for three comments: (1) it was his first visit to Italy; (2) the modest reporting of Octave's performance in the French press – four lines in L'Auto, giving the names of the top three riders – does not reveal whether Lapize travelled alone or with team-mates. It is not even quite clear whether he was still riding for Biguet or already with Alcyon; (3) it was not until the next day that Lapize was declared the victor following Ganna's disqualification for 'boxing him in outrageously' in the sprint. Commentators emphasized the fair play displayed by the Italian Cycling Union in being prepared to take this brave decision in Varese, Ganna's heartland.

thing was that Lapize and three other riders had left the official route and taken another, shorter by three or four kilometres. The regulations were applied posthaste: the first four riders were disqualified and victory passed to the fifth-placed man, who had reached Tours 12 minutes behind Lapize. Since this was Faber, it was still a success for Alcyon. That day, Calais and Baugé were laughing, winners both on the road and by default. Monsieur Gentil was doubly pleased.

It fell to the Tour of Lombardy to close the season. This was a good race for the French, the most recent winners being Faber and Garrigou. Alcyon, which had designs on the Italian market, decided to send its strongest team. But how would they get there? By bike, of course: in four stages. Lapize was enlisted for this Italian job which went by way of Dijon, Chambéry and Turin. He enjoyed the trip greatly, and the group's high spirits: in Chambéry, Trousselier won a personal triumph in a *fromage frais* fight in which Octave was judged to be 'pretty handy'.

In Milan, the party continued. The Tour of Lombardy was billed as an extraordinary meeting, a Herculean trial. The race organiser, *Gazzetta dello Sport*, had dreamed up the idea of opening the race to all-comers, and 415 riders turned up at the start in Milan for a race over an easy 210-kilometre route. Six hours later, a 45-strong peloton emerged into utter chaos in Sesto San Giovanni, on the outskirts of Milan 'where the finish was judged – or rather where the finish was not judged straight away.' In a huge crowd, the Italian champion Cuniolo was declared the victor ahead of Trousselier, and that was that. The rest of the rankings were only known the next day; Lapize had come fourth. The special correspondent from *L'Auto* politely regretted that there had been nothing to indicate the final kilometre, and consequently the French riders had started sprinting far too early.

As chance would have it, the special correspondent that day was Robert Desmarets, and on the same page as his report, *L'Auto* published a photograph of the construction of the Vel d'Hiv' (Winter Velodrome) in Paris. The funny thing is that a little later on, Robert 'Bob' Desmarets would be appointed Director of the Vel d'Hiv'.

Coming back to our story, 7 November saw the close of the 1909 road racing season. It was rumoured, then confirmed by the American organisers, that Lapize and three other French riders were being invited to compete in the New York Six Days.

The scandalised Belgians cried foul. They were ignored.

Octave freed one place by not taking up the invitation. He had just celebrated his 22nd birthday, and wisely retired to the family seat in Villiers-sur-Marne. Octave senior savoured the moment.

DUEL ON THE TOUR

On 13 February 1910, Paris saw a significant event which showed that track cycling still had the upper hand over road racing. That day, the brand new Vélodrome d'Hiver opened its doors for a two-day inauguration programme. The races on offer were reserved exclusively for sprinters and motor-paced 'stayers': the kings of speed. Those who did not make it on the track became 'slaves of the road', and were not invited to the Vel d'Hiv on the Rue Nélaton.

Anyway, Paris was happy to have its smart new winter track at last – and in such a prestigious location (at Métro station Grenelle, just down the road from the Eiffel Tower!). The famous flood of the Seine and an epidemic of strikes had delayed its opening and heightened the impatience of the sporting public. Hitherto, the winter races had retreated to a miserable warehouse at the Galerie des Machines, a temporary construction put up at the same time as the no less temporary Eiffel Tower, for the 1889 Universal Exhibition. This is how the revue *La Vie au Grand Air* (Outdoor Life) greeted the occasion:

> The Machine Gallery had its own charm, it must be said. We got in the habit of going there every time bad weather kept us from the open-air velodromes. But this indoor track was dirty, sullen and nausea-inducing. The Palais des Sports (the other name for the Vel d'Hiv) on the other hand, is full of laughter, stylish and pleasant. You have the feeling that the dullest of races could become exciting there. The public, full of enthusiasm for the new velodrome – the Palace of Sports, the Palace of Light – went home

regretting that the delayed opening had robbed it of some fine spectacles. But they will make up for it from now on.

We will see later on how things went at the famous Vel d'Hiv.

For now, at the beginning of 1910, Messieurs Peugeot and Desgrange were still at loggerheads, which was bad news – but the good news was that the La Française-Diamant team was back on the road after several years' absence. Finally, the strange news was to be found in the racing calendar. This season would begin with Paris–Roubaix, a week before Milan–San Remo.

Paris–Roubaix, the Easter Race – hence its moveable date, 17 March that year – remained Paris–Roubaix: the start in Chatou, the climb at Doullens, the cobblestones in Hénin-Liétard,* the so-called cycle tracks, and a little over 260 kilometres. But, though the race had not changed, Octave Lapize was a different man. The dark horse of 1909 had become the bookies' favourite and the trump card in a hand containing three or four other aces of equal value. The Alcyon team was a formidable machine, with considerable resources at its disposal. Octave Lapize, who had known lean times with Biguet, was no doubt amazed to discover the details of the operation worked out by the racing service of his new team.

It was huge. For Alcyon, Paris–Roubaix began at 8pm on the Saturday evening in a big *brasserie* on the Avenue de la Grande-Armée (my witness called it 'a large avenue between the Porte Maillot and the Étoile,' as if he was afraid of betraying a secret). A dozen masseurs and *soigneurs* prepared both the food for the race and the pre-race meal planned for 3am, by which time the head chef and his assistants were in full swing. They lit the gas beneath the 100 eggs – poached, fried and omelettes – which the racers would gulp down to follow their hot broth. They brought out gigantic platters loaded with cold meats, dishes

---

* Now Hénin-Beaumont.

bearing appetizing rice puddings, vast canisters of coffee, tea and hot milk. For the race itself, gleaming new tin flasks were filled with hot chocolate, coffee, creamed rice, chicken stock and mineral water. A mountain of sandwiches was constructed from copiously buttered hunks of bread filled with ham, cheese, omelette and various jams, and the impressive menu was completed by succulent pieces of chicken, cutlets, fruit tarts, bananas, figs, prunes, bars of chocolate and packets of sugar.

A short distance away stood a selection of drinks from which the racers could choose to go with their meal, according to individual taste. One of them slowly tasted the contents of his two flasks with little sips then, scowling, examined the cap of each, which bore the label 'sweet coffee with a small glass of fine champagne (cognac)'. On reading this he exclaimed furiously, in a working-class Paris drawl, 'No way! Now they're holding back the good stuff. What a place!' He called a waiter and ordered him to look lively and pour another little glass of 'fine champagne' into each of his coffee flasks.

There were a few rough diamonds and some seasoned campaigners in young Octave's circle.

Octave himself arrived at kilometre zero in Chatou looking focused but without any apparent anxiety. And wouldn't you know it, his self-assurance was justified when 270 kilometres, nine hours, five minutes and 12 seconds later, Octave Lapize won in Roubaix for the second time. This time he dominated the event, taking a firm grip on the race from one end to the other. Summing up, the papers reported that 'the marvellous star of our two great houses Alcyon and Dunlop went at an average of 29.96 kph, a superb performance given that the wind was against him.' But the most striking thing is that the ace of 1910 was not the same man as the novice of 1909. In front of journalists, he allowed himself a 'Phew! I did it,' and told the story of his day confidently and eloquently: 'There were 60 of us in Beauvais, and still 60 in Amiens. Very few had dropped off before Doullens. But that was where the famous climb was going to sort out the field. I went up in front at full tilt and, at the top when I looked back, there were only nine of us left. It began to get serious when a *pédard* [a common cyclist] got in my way and I had to swerve, and fell. I managed to close the gap before Arras and, without losing a second, I broke away from all the rest.' The shrewd tactician allowed himself to be caught again because they were pressing strongly behind him and because he knew that the cobbles themselves would sort them out. First Faber, then Georget and Vandenberghe and finally Crupperlandt were dropped. Lapize can finish the story: 'There were just four of us as we came into the velodrome. I let Vanhouwaert lead. At 300 metres I drew level and feigned an attack. The Belgian fell for it and started sprinting. Of course, when I really attacked him as we went into the straight, he had no answer and I passed him easily.'

How nicely put. The classification confirms that Vanhouwaert was second by two lengths and Christophe by three. Léonard was several seconds behind, in fourth. What's most obvious is that the top four finishers belonged to the same Alcyon team and that none of these four had made any concession to his team-mates. Either on the road or the track.

The cannier riders at Alcyon very quickly realized that if they wanted first place in the race, they needed to come first in the team.

In Milan–San Remo the following Sunday, Lapize and Vanhouwaert, having understood the situation, were the first to attack at Novi Ligure. In apocalyptic conditions, the rain turning to snow, they sliced through a road that was turning into a stream of mud. As the snow thickened, the riders melted away. Eugène Christophe, the undisputed cyclo-cross champion, was in his element and caught the pair of escapees with Ganna, the Italian favourite. First Lapize, then Vanhouwaert, a little further on, gave up. The race would become legend. Of 72 starters, only four riders made it through to San Remo. Christophe, the victor, beat second-placed Ganna by 40 minutes! It was a famous victory for the valiant French rider, but a bitter one: according to his own account, Christophe needed more than a year to recover. Fifty years later, when I asked him to describe his ordeal, he always began the story with the words, 'Wait a minute. I can still feel the cold in my bones.'

The season continued. The first of May was Paris–Brussels and the next day's newspapers describe a perfect re-run of Paris–Roubaix. In short, 'Another French victory. In the fifth Paris–Brussels, Lapize beats Vanhouwaert by a length... Six in the sprint... Belgians on the podium... A triumph over the entire course... Eight Alcyon men among the first ten places, including the top four.'

Here endeth the lesson. Octave Lapize had proven strongest. But then crafty old Brocco, who had finished seventh by eight minutes, lodged a complaint on the grounds that the six leaders had not respected the five-minute neutralization at the final control point in Gembloux, 30 kilometres from the finish (he himself had taken refuge in a café). His complaint was judged to be valid and the classification revised. Brocco, it turned out, was the victor in the Paris–Brussels won by Lapize, who in the end was given second place, while the Legnano brand that equipped Brocco arrived too late to gain any publicity.

Octave missed out on Bordeaux–Paris. He abandoned the French championship which was held in conditions reminiscent of the Milan–San Remo. Was he keeping his powder dry? It is possible, because the big event that had so caught his imagination the previous year was approaching. And this particular Tour de France was being billed as nothing short of monstrous: for the first time, the course would not join the Mediterranean and Atlantic coasts by a straight line through Toulouse, but swerve into the Pyrenees and follow the whole range from East to West, from Perpignan to Bayonne.

Sent to reconnoitre the course in May, Alphonse Steinès had reassured Desgrange of the good quality of the mountain roads. He was lying, of course, having lost his way in the snow. He had embellished these shoddy tracks by naming his course the 'Route des Thermes', but Petit-Breton and other riders who had decided to take a closer look for themselves were talking about the 'Circle of Death'. This may not have been panic, exactly, but it wasn't far off.

To distract attention on the eve of the *Grand Départ*, Henri Desgrange let off a firework. He criticized François Faber, the outright winner of 1909, for a lack of seriousness, favouring Lapize, whom he tipped for victory in Paris.

And so was heralded the Faber-Lapize duel. It was going to last 29 days and would be fought over 4,474 kilometres.

This intense, implacable combat took place between 3 and 31 July 1910. We can experience it ('live' as they say nowadays) as vividly as if it were happening today. First of all, we have the accounts of witnesses waxing lyrical, and anecdotes designed to feed the epic myth. These subjective documents appeal mainly to our feelings and imagination. But there is another more objective representation of the duel in the form of a diagram sketched by an unemotional analyst. On a white sheet of paper, a dry-point pen traces the two protagonists' simultaneous trajectories: two lines that quickly diverge, then are broken, bisect each other, become entangled, but which in the end are distinct and not without their own elegance. This diagram, reflecting cold logic and calculation, in its own way reflects the sheer grim relentlessness of the duel.

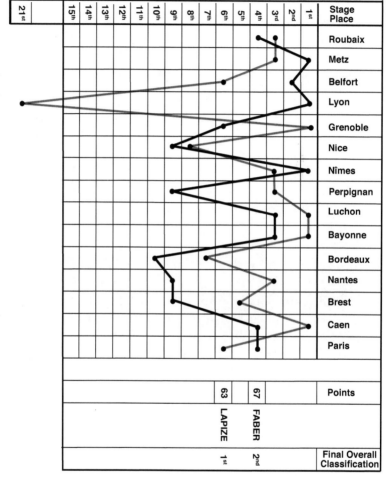

Four stage wins, finally victorious despite the disaster at Lyon.

N.B. Each rider's points total was revised at the end of Stage 9, and again before the final stage, to take account of those riders who had been eliminated.

A duel must naturally be fought by the rules – in this case, the regulations of the Tour de France. These stated that, as in previous years, classification was by points and not by time; the winner of each stage gained one point, the second-placed rider two, and so on.

Each rider only received one point more than the man in front of him, whether they arrived at the same time or thirty minutes apart. The ultimate winner, then, would be the one with the fewest points at the finish in Paris.

Out of the 110 racers at the start, 29 were *groupés* (riding in teams) and 81 *isolés* (individuals). The *groupés*, who were the best riders, were divided into three teams: Alcyon, Le Globe, which had only managed to rustle together nine competitors instead of ten, and Legnano.

The Italian team had been vigorously reinforced by the Peugeot team's champions. Monsieur Peugeot was still giving *L'Auto* the cold shoulder, but gave his riders free reign to enter in a personal capacity.

Here is the the list of the 29 *groupés*, and the only real contenders.

Riding for Alcyon were Faber, the previous year's winner, at No. 1, followed by Garrigou, twice runner-up already, and Trousselier, the 1905 winner. Lapize, the little prodigy, wore No.4. Then came other respected riders such as the Belgians Vanhouwaert and Blaise, Godivier, Cadolle, Léonard and Bettini.

For Legnano, Petit-Breton, the winner in 1907 and 1908 was naturally the leader. He was surrounded by the Frenchmen Brocco, Dartignacq, Émile Georget and Ménager, and four Italians, Albini, the brothers Ernesto and Paul Azzini and finally Bordin.

Le Globe fielded lesser stars and less lofty ambitions in Cornet, the 1904 victor, and Cruppelandt, accompanied by Beaugendre, Paulmier, Maitron, Lannoy, Deloffre, Loit and Saillot (Lapize's ex-team-mate at Biguet).

The first surprise was that Le Globe set off at a gallop. Cruppelandt hailed from Roubaix, and had the good taste to take the first Paris–Roubaix stage. Not in the sprint, as he had done before, but with a lead of 15 minutes over those gentlemen from Alcyon: Vanhouwaert, Lapize and Faber, in that order. As the second stage began, from Roubaix to Metz, Faber was keen to make Desgrange eat his words.* He attacked, attacked again and arrived alone, seven minutes ahead of Garrigou and Lapize. The classification read: first, Faber with five points; second, Lapize with six. Somewhat doleful, Desgrange went back slightly on his original forecast. He was right to do so, because in the third Metz-Belfort stage, by way of the Ballon d'Alsace, Faber finished second and moved up another four points over Lapize, who appeared shaken. Octave was able to reassure his followers, explaining that on the descent from the Col du Ballon (which he crossed in second place behind the stage winner, Émile Georget) he had ridden over a bottle and lost his tyre! Whatever the whys and wherefores, though, Lapize went from seeming shaken to being properly sunk in the fourth stage from Belfort to Lyon. Lapize began to sulk. Relations between him and Vanhouwaert were strained (perhaps the Belgian was a bit fed up with being beaten by one or two lengths whenever they met in a sprint). That day, the two riders held each other back 'solely in order not to give ground to the other', and finished 20th and 21st respectively. François Faber put a good cushion between himself and his rivals by winning his second stage and nicely bolstering his lead in the general classification.

---

* Metz, a German town since 1871, welcomed the Tour from 1907. Planned for 4 o'clock, or 5 o'clock German time, the finish was on a marvellous terrace a kilometre long, looking out over the Moselle valley and containing the most exquisite Roman garden imaginable, and all of it framing a statue of Wilhelm I, grandfather of the current Emperor. A significant number of police officers kept order admirably. Nonetheless, in 1911, Longwy took Metz's place as a ville-étape. In 1919, the Tour de France would return to Metz, now a French town once more.

This time it was Lapize's turn to come in for criticism from Desgrange, who was unaware of what everyone in the peloton knew: for two days, young Octave had been suffering with such terrible pain in his feet that no-one would have been surprised had he abandoned the race altogether. The Tour de France was only a quarter of the way through and some perfidious observers were starting to suggest that the real duel was going to be between Faber and Georget.

And now it was into the Alps with the fifth stage from Lyon to Grenoble, via Geneva. Lapize gritted his teeth, choked back his tears and tucked in behind the Legnano riders Petit-Breton and Azzini, who had decided to climb the Col de Cerdon flat out. And what happened next? Faber, with a cold on an off day and Georget, with violent stomach pains, were dropped straight away. In front, they kept up the pace and Lapize and the others worked hard to tidy up. In Geneva, Faber's group was four and a half minutes behind. By Annecy, the gap had grown to 10 minutes. At the foot of the Col de Porte, there were just seven riders in the leaders' group.

Then what? Lapize and Vanhouwaert found themselves shoulder to shoulder as the thunder roared and the rain poured, and the road surface suddenly deteriorated dreadfully. This time there was no trickery; in the words of Desgrange, 'They rode brilliantly, like men possessed.' Vanhouwaert refused to let his feet touch the ground on his way up the terrible ramp, while Lapize alternated between riding and running. It was Lapize's method that paid off, although he was unexpectedly overtaken at the summit by Cruppelandt, coming from behind. On the descent towards Grenoble, Lapize's feet were hurting more and more, but he kept pressing because Vanhouwaert was breathing down his neck again. And then? Vanhouwaert, at that moment the 'Lion of Flanders' as never before, exploded through the storm and caught Lapize. Flying like the wind and rain, they charged at breakneck speed and were closing the gap on Cruppelandt at Le Sappey when Vanhouwaert punctured and stopped. A little further down, Lapize also punctured – and did not stop. On his rims, he passed Cruppelandt and arrived in Grenoble at the bend of the Chemin de Latronche. It was only 1:30pm, and the champions were not expected until 2:30. Latecomers were in for a disappointment. A bugle sounded and Lapize appeared at the end of the final straight. He made as if to sprint, but it was obvious that there was a problem: his rear tube was flat. Thunderous applause greeted his victory, his first in the Tour de France. He did not so much dismount as drop from the saddle, and hurled his shoes away. We will never know how much energy it must have cost the valiant rider, whose feet were suffering so terribly. But the show at the finishing line was not yet over. From the first to the 44th place, the survivors limped in one by one. Five hours elapsed between the arrival of Lapize and that of Wiringer, in 62nd and last place.

In his socks, with a new reputation as a top-class climber, Lapize hobbled painfully to his hotel. By winning the stage, he had risen to third place overall. François Faber, courageous in the extreme, finished at 22 minutes but still in sixth place, retaining his position as leader. The duel announced at the start was still valid, but somewhat complicated by the presence of Garrigou in second place and Vanhouwaert, tying in third with Lapize. With four Alcyon riders in the top four places, triumph for the brand was guaranteed, but worries were just starting to set in for its management. Calais and Baugé, the manager and *directeur sportif*, spent the rest day wondering how to maintain the team's cohesion. As for Lapize, he concentrated on repairing his feet with the help of his *soigneur*, Stoffer.

In the Grenoble-Nice stage, Octave was full of beans, though victory evaded him due to an untimely puncture. His eighth place was not a disaster, since Faber was ninth. It was even a point gained.

Between the Alps and the Pyrenees, the race was most remarkable for its incidents. On the rest day in Nice, the Tour de France had its first death to lament. An individual rider, the Breton Adolphe Hélière, died from shock after jumping into the sea to bathe.

Between Nice and Nîmes, yet another puncture prevented Lapize from contesting the stage victory. He finished at four minutes – which was not important – and third, which was not the end of the world, except that first place had gone to Faber: two points lost.

In the stage from Nîmes to Perpignan, a long breakaway by Paulmier and Maitron surprised everyone: they went all the way to the finish without being caught, at the vertiginous average of 34.6 kph. When the peloton arrived, it was to contest third place, which went to Lapize. This was a very profitable result for Octave, because it was Faber's turn to fall victim to a puncture, and he dropped six points by only coming ninth. Faber still led the overall classification with 33 points to Lapize's 48. But what about Garrigou? Garrigou was nowhere to be seen. He had suddenly lost 25 points following an inexplicable fall. But who would dare call it inexplicable to Garrigou's face? Gustave angrily blamed the fall on the fact that 'somebody' had tampered with his machine, loosening his lock-nuts. And he had a suspicion that this 'somebody' belonged to team Alcyon. After Perpignan, it was noted by everyone that, rightly or wrongly, Garrigou did not look the same way at Faber again. Was it really possible?*

---

* One day in 1960, I had the good fortune to meet Gustave Garrigou and to hear his version of these events. 'As every evening, I had taken care to bring my bicycle up to my room after the Nîmes stage. It might seem a pointless precaution because we Alcyon riders had dominated that year's Tour from the start. But there wasn't much love lost between us. Anyway, that evening I forgot to lock my bedroom door, and this mistake, for that's what it was, cost me dear. It was 3am and we were crossing Lunel when my wheel suddenly gave way, ball bearings all over the road. A nice job, you could say. The cap had been unscrewed and I hadn't noticed a thing. I had to find a mechanic, and more importantly ball bearings of the right gauge. Frankly, I lost an hour and 30 minutes thanks to that accident. At the time, I was only a few points behind Faber.' At this point in his story, Gustave Garrigou paused. And, in the same calm voice, he told me: 'Mark you, Faber didn't win that Tour. Lapize was the winner. I have to say that was the moment I had my revenge. Not because Faber had sabotaged my bike. Absolutely not. It's just that Lapize won.'

But the immensity of the task ahead quelled the rumours and calmed the spirits. The Pyrenees had arrived, threatening to turn everything upside-down. And so it was. In Perpignan, it was reported euphemistically that Garrigou had had a serious technical problem. In Bayonne, it had become a disgraceful assassination attempt. You see what I mean?

There was much rejoicing as Perpignan celebrated its first Tour. At the start of the stage, which would finish at Luchon, the sporting public started gathering in the Place de l'Arago at two o'clock in the morning. The start was not due until half past three, but there was a great crush as everyone came to cheer each of the 62 valiant riders still in the race. The question on everyone's mind that night was a simple one: if there were 62 in Perpignan, how many would there be at Luchon after the terrible climbs and terrifying drops of the Col de Porte, the Portet d'Aspet and the Ares? Perhaps it was the fear of being alone on unknown roads, but there were no significant developments until Foix, where the peloton stopped for two minutes at the control point. The riders used this time to change their gear ratios. All the riders, that is, except Lapize, who took the risk of retaining a higher gear.

I would like to pause and reflect for a moment. I ask you to imagine the state of mountain paths in 1910 and at the same time to believe that the gradients of the Portet-d'Aspet were no less than they are today. Well, ladies and gentlemen, Lapize wanted to cross the Portet d'Aspet and the entire stage on a 65 inch gear: that is, a ratio of 22x9 (nowadays 41x17 or 46x19). Lapize's phenomenal 65 inch gear was confirmed by Petit-Breton himself (after his abandonment, Petit-Breton followed the race for *La Vie au Grand Air*). Nowadays, on the Portet-d'Aspet, racers opt for a 53 inch gear.

Back to the business in hand. It should be said that on the Portet, Émile Georget, with a lower gear, led Lapize a merry dance, but the latter held on well and even managed to go clear by not stopping at the final control point. He would not be seen again. He crossed the Col des Ares at a gallop and arrived in

Luchon with a lead of eight minutes. Here is what Desgrange had to say:

> I wish to tell you once again that Lapize will be the true revelation of this eighth Tour de France... His masterly approach to the stage, his superb surge up the Portet-d'Aspet and on the Col des Ares constitute feats that bring him the highest honour and class him among the greatest road riders we have ever seen... Lapize is not much to look at, but behind his fragile appearance lie genuine energy and exceptional ability. So it is with great warmth that I cry: 'Bravo, Lapize!'

Bravo to Lapize, then, but Faber was still hanging on well, arriving third in Luchon (though by a full fifteen minutes). And it was Desgrange's conviction that, even though he was incontestably the more brilliant rider, Lapize would not be able to wrest first place from Faber, whom he tipped as favourite for the Tourmalet stage. But just because Henri Desgrange was the boss of the Tour, it did not mean he knew everything. He did not know, for instance, that Octave had confided to his deputy (and the president of Octave's old club), Alphonse Steinès, that he had saved plenty of strength for the stage to come.

Between ourselves, I would say that Desgrange was in a pretty bad mood. For him, it was intolerable that 59 of the 62 riders who had left Perpignan had made it to Luchon. Steinès reassured him, predicting 50% wastage between Luchon and Bayonne. Did somebody say wastage? The first man dropped out even before the starting pistol had fired: Henri Desgrange himself, feeling off-colour, decided to go straight back to Paris, leaving Victor Breyer to take the reins. The reasons for this abandonment have never been explained. Some of the more mischievous observers claimed that Desgrange was scared of losing the Tour on the Tourmalet. But the race – and the riders – carried on.

At two o'clock on the morning of 21 July 1910, the party was in full swing on the Allées d'Étigny in Luchon. The Thermes

Casino provided the entertainment. Never had there been such a spectacle. The Tour de France would certainly be coming back to Luchon.

However, at half past three in the morning, the first climb could just be seen, rising up beyond the end of the Allées d'Étigny: the Col de Peyresourde. The night was silent. Every man knew that after the first climb there would be a second, the Col d'Aspin, then a third, the Tourmalet, a fourth, the Col du Soulor, a fifth, the Col de Tortes (a pass which disappeared from the road atlas around 1920), a sixth, the Col d'Aubisque and finally a seventh, the Col d'Osquich. In the darkness, they climbed rapidly. At the summit of Peyresourde, after climbing the 15 kilometres in 58 minutes, Lapize and Garrigou were out in front. Faber had trouble getting under way and did not figure among the first 30 riders. No-one rated the chances of the Giant of Colombes very highly.

As they approached the Col d'Aspin – it was not quite five o'clock in the morning, but the Vallée d'Aure was thronged with spectators – the race started to take shape. Lapize and Garrigou led the dance, with a lead of four minutes over a group of six riders, including an *isolé* who was inspiring enthusiastic support as the local boy of the stage. He was said to come from Bayonne, although he actually hailed from Lahontan, a village not far from Salies-de-Béarn. He knew the Pyrenees, then, and especially the Aubisque region. The other surprise at the foot of the Aspin was that Faber had managed to limit the damage. He passed at nine minutes and in ninth place. On the slopes of the Aspin, the onlookers were treated to a duel 'between two wild men', Garrigou and Lapize, battling tooth and nail. Half-way up, with a supple and powerful turn of his pedals, Lapize, still with a higher gear than his opponent, took off on his own and crossed the summit in the lead by three minutes. He did not press the advantage, though, and Garrigou, tearing down on the descent, caught him at Sainte-Marie-de-Campan.

Now, the Tourmalet, third step in the Giants' Staircase, was upon them. On the 17-kilometre ascent, Lapize and Garrigou would abandon themselves to another fierce battle lasting an hour and a half. At the fifth kilometre, Lapize established a lead of 100 metres, then 200, which quickly stretched to 500 metres. It was all over, it seemed. But after some furious pedal strokes that 'lifted him out of the saddle', Octave dismounted and covered the next 100 metres on foot.* Behind him, Garrigou showed no intention of giving up. Ten times, twenty times he looked as though he was about to fall, but stayed in the saddle. His 55 inch gear was better than Lapize's 59 inch, but still the equivalent of 45x22 or 39x19, which no-one would dare to risk today! With a desperate effort, Garrigou kept his balance to become the first man ever to climb the whole of the Tourmalet by bicycle, and to win the special bonus of 100 francs put up by Burton, the distinguished sporting enthusiast.

But Garrigou's bravery could not prevent Lapize from arriving first at the summit, having once again alternated running and cycling. Beneath the Touring Club's sign displaying the altitude of 2,122m, the spectators – drivers and cyclists alike – were dumbfounded. The sun was starting to make itself felt. It was 7:30am and the racers were arriving right on time: unbelievable! The Italian Albini passed in third, ahead of Cruchon – and Lafourcade: unthinkable! Faber once again clocked in at nine minutes. Still, certain reporters, as well as the new man in charge, Victor Breyer, were worried. By the Tourmalet, there were just 70 kilometres on the clock. Another 256 kilometres left to Bayonne.

On the descent, at Barèges, Garrigou caught Lapize and further on, at Argelès-Gazost, Albini managed to join them as well. He had come back too quickly, however, and on the first slopes of the Col du Soulor, he was dropped. A little higher up, Garrigou paid for his efforts on the Tourmalet and let Lapize, who was showing signs of fatigue himself, slip through his fingers. Octave really was feeling faint, as

---

* No-one who witnessed this famous scene dared to use the expression 'danseuse'.

the massacre continued. This was when the *isolé* Lafourcade suddenly appeared. The local rider knew the slopes and had come equipped with the right gears. With his 52 inch gear (still 39x20, mind you), he left all the top riders standing and crossed the Soulor, the Tortes and the Aubisque in the lead. Behind him, there was a long silence. Victor Breyer was horrified, starting to think that everybody else had given up. But, after a quarter of an hour, a lone rider appeared at the last bend. Recognizing Lapize, Breyer breathed again. He walked towards him and, as always at times like these, asked a stupid question: 'Well now, Lapize, what's wrong?' Then Lapize let fly the most famous retort in the history of the Tour de France. 'You're murderers!' shouted Lapize. 'That's what's wrong. You're criminals!'

Sixteen minutes had passed since Lafourcade had come by. It was 10:30, very hot, and there were another 180 kilometres to go. The survivors hauled themselves one by one to the top of the Aubisque, where observers ticked off Albini, Cruppelandt, Trousselier and Cruchon. Faber, lying in seventh place, was 41 minutes off the lead.

It was Albini's turn to try a solo effort. At Oloron, he came across Lapize, and dropped him. He came back up to Lafourcade and dropped him as well. In Mauléon, just imagine: it was an Italian, of all people, who was leading the way. Albini only slipped up on the last step of the Giants' Staircase: the paltry Col d'Osquich, which only just manages 500 metres above sea level. At the same moment, Octave Lapize regained some strength. He caught Albini at St-Jean-Pied-de-Port. 30 kilometres from Bayonne, the two escapees decided to join forces, or what was left of them, to get themselves to the end of the ordeal. It was just as well, because now it was François Faber's turn for a solo effort. Despite three punctures, he passed first Cruppelandt, then Cruchon. He joined Trousselier and Lafourcade and swept them along with him at a furious speed. By Cambo, François the Great had halved his deficit since the Aubisque to 24 minutes.

In Bayonne, a cheering crowd saw Lapize beat Albini in the sprint. Twenty minutes later, an utterly delirious crowd surged onto the road to give Lafourcade a hero's welcome, a valiant fifth behind Faber and Trousselier. The riders were drunk with fatigue, the race followers with the day's images, and the spectators with delight. In Desgrange's absence, Victor Breyer editorialized: 'It's improbable! It's madness! It's unheard-of! It's everything you could wish for!'

A little later, the statistics came through. Lapize had covered the 326 kilometres in fourteen hours and two minutes: an average of more than 23 kph. Having started at 3:30am, he arrived at 5:40 in the afternoon, at the same time as a telegram reporting the arrival of other competitors in Mauléon, 90 kilometres from the finish. Optimistic officials announced a beautiful full moon, a stroke of luck for the last arrivals who would be pedalling after dusk. On learning the latest news in Paris, a magnanimous Desgrange decided that the times would be overlooked. Every one of the 41 riders who reached Bayonne would be allowed to continue the Tour.

At his hotel, Octave Lapize was tending his feet, which were nicely inflamed from his runs up the scree-strewn slopes of the Tourmalet and Aubisque. Totting up the day's results, it was hard for him to accept that he had gone through all that for just two paltry points on Faber, who was still nine points ahead in the general classification. The duel was about to enter its final phase, with Faber leading by thirty-two points to forty-one. For Lapize, there were only five more chances to attack and make up the gap. Faber just needed to hold out five more times to preserve his lead.

Octave was convinced that victory would come to the one who could hold his nerve best. To get a better evening's rest, he decided to take his dinner in his room.

The stage from Bayonne to Bordeaux was a short one at 268 kilometres, and a straightforward one, but the start was set for 3:30am in order to give the Bordeaux public a lunchtime finish. Nobody had time to complain because the entire peloton – or almost – was about to be plunged into a cyclist's nightmare that had not been seen for several years: nails. Just as in the time of the first Tours de France, practical jokers had strewn nails across the road. Four riders managed to avoid the trap and rode all the way to Bordeaux without being caught. In the sprint, however, Cruppelandt, who was without doubt the fastest, was judged to have boxed Azzini in and was relegated, leaving the stage win to Ernest Paul. This was no ordinary rider: firstly, he was racing as an independent; second, he was riding an Alcyon bicycle; and third, he was François Faber's half-brother.

The manner of his win might have set tongues wagging, but at the finishing line the main topic of conversation was the carnage caused by the nails in the early part of the race. Lapize had the better luck in this dirty business: he had to stop only three times. As for Faber, he suffered four punctures, the last of them not far from the finish. He took tenth spot in Bordeaux, to Lapize's seventh. Three points changed hands. The table read: 1st Faber, 42 points. 2nd Lapize, 48 points. His brother's victory was not enough to calm Faber's nerves.

Especially since the Alcyon team, if not actually split, had diverged. Baugé had taken charge of Faber while Calais looked after Lapize. Quite an atmosphere in the dressing room.

Faber was the more nervous at the meeting point, the Quatre Pavillons, for a 2am start, because the Bordeaux-Nantes stage was 391 kilometres long. Big François had decided to use strong-arm tactics and scatter his opponents by leading an almost lone charge, at a horrific pace. He ate up the kilometres at an average of 31 per hour with an escort of no more than a dozen riders, one of whom, of course, was Lapize. The wits had a whale of a time, some of them not hesitating to point out cleverly that of the two duelists it was Faber who was riding like a deaf man. Alas, the Luxembourger was also wearing blinkers. In Marans, he crashed into a dog and flew over his handlebars. Everything was in pieces: Faber had injured his legs, hands and head, and his bicycle was in a sorry state: both wheels buckled, just an axle where a pedal should have been, and the handlebars bent double. The 'Giant of Colombes' burst into tears. It was fully 20 minutes before he could leave again. But something inexplicable and marvellous happened.

Within 80 kilometres, Faber took back 16 minutes from his former companions, who were travelling at 20 kph. Lapize himself did nothing to increase the pace. At La Roche-sur-Yon, the Alcyon mechanics repaired Faber's bicycle and he resumed his place at the head of the race. There was relief all round – for a while – until Garrigou sparked off a new crisis with a devastating attack. The wits – still there – recalled the Nîmes-Perpignan incident, and suggested with a snigger that Gustave had decided to 'tighten the screws'. The group broke away in an instant. Lapize gritted his teeth and hitched himself to the right wagon. Faber burst into tears once more and arrived in Nantes 15 minutes after the leaders. Trousselier, Vanhouwaert, Garrigou, Lapize and Bettini – all from the Alcyon team – came in in that order, demonstrating that no-one was giving anything away in favour of comrade Octave. Faber could only manage ninth place, having lost five points in the scuffle. The scoreboard began to flash: 1st Faber, 51 points. 2nd Lapize, 52 points. The two men were neck and neck. The duel was getting fiercer.

The next day's weather was dreadful: it poured for 321 kilometres, all the way from Nantes to Brest. Rumours of Faber's abandonment were exaggerated: he was at the start. A moderate pace was set as far as Châteaulin, where Garrigou again decided to step on the gas. It took everyone by surprise, shook them, even. Faber and Lapize themselves seemed to be in some difficulty, particularly the latter. That, at least, was Faber's assessment as he attacked and put some distance between himself and his rival. In actual fact, Lapize was playing dead. He came back on the Luxembourger and counter-attacked before Landerneau. This was the moment that the great Faber cracked completely and began to cry. An exhausted Garrigou finally had his stage win, but that was just a sideshow. Lapize, not exactly frisky himself, snatched fifth place. A tearful Faber arrived in ninth.

With two stages left until the finish, the top places had switched. For the first time, Lapize was in front of Faber, with a three-point lead.

In Brest, both men spent the rest day recuperating. Though they were equally tired, Lapize seemed to be winning the psychological battle.

But it was as well to be wary of a wounded animal, expecially when the animal's name was Faber. The great François attacked from the very start of the Brest-Caen stage. And Lapize cracked. In Saint-Brieuc, still riding furiously, Faber had a lead of 20 minutes, but then fell victim to two punctures himself. He lost his cool, floundered and was caught in Dinan by Ernest Paul, (who had been riding behind, not really where a brother ought to be), by the ubiquitous Vanhouwaert and the inevitable Lapize, who was really pleased to have come back from such a distance. The race thinned out when Vanhouwaert disappeared thanks to a puncture. But it exploded again on the climb at Sartilly, after Granville, with another attack from the irrepressible Garrigou. Lapize and Ernest Paul managed to keep contact, but Faber was dropped, stranded. In dire straits, he lost 12 minutes in 15 kilometres. In Caen, he arrived 40 minutes behind the three leaders, but still managed to take fourth place. It would not have been so serious if Lapize had not come first. It turned out that Octave had beaten Garrigou and Ernest Paul in the sprint. He had also taken the lead in terms of stage wins, with four to Faber's three, and had extended his lead in the general classification. Following a last painstaking revision, this declared: 1st Lapize, 57 points. 2nd Faber, 63 points. 3rd Garrigou, 78 points. All three Alcyon riders.

All was well at Alcyon, then? Don't you believe it. Alcyon was keeping a low profile. At the finishing line, Baugé attempted to fend off the journalists when his champions arrived. He dreaded an off-the-cuff remark in a moment of exhaustion, or a barbed comment in the heat of the moment about a team-mate's behaviour.

Faber was feverish and in no mood to talk to the press. Lapize might have wanted to indulge in a spot of banter, but held himself back. During the rest day, two doctors took it in turns to attend the bedside of the vanquished champion in an attempt to get him back on his feet. Lapize, meanwhile, was going strong. He intended to make the most of the aviation festival being held in Caen to take a trip in an aeroplane. People wondered about the reasons for this surprising excursion at such a crucial point in the race. Was it Lapize wanting to rub it in and show Faber how relaxed he was, or was he genuinely smitten with flying? People would have to wait four years to find out. For now, the newspapers had a field day and the cover of *La Vie au Grand Air* was given over to a photo of Lapize in the cockpit with Morane, holder of the air speed record.

At seven o'clock the next morning, half an hour later than planned because a favourable wind was forecast, Lapize had to come back down to earth. He had hardly left when a puncture stopped him in his tracks. Faber didn't let sentimentality hold him back. He put his foot down and took with him seven riders who were in a hurry to get to Paris. The Parc des Princes was 260 kilometres away, and Lapize had been dropped, with no hope of coming back. And this is how it stood at Deauville: at the head of the race Faber, Ernest Paul, Paulmier, Ménager, Cruppelandt, Vanhouwaert, Bettini and the Italian Azzini. Lapize, isolated in a group of *isolés* was already eight minutes behind, and the rain continued to fall. By Rouen, the halfway point, the gap had widened to 12 minutes and the rain was showing no signs of abating. The race was changing course, as some riders were dropped from the front and others caught at the back. In front, Paulmier and Vanhouwaert were unable to keep up, and the lead of Faber's group had shrunk to just six minutes. At the same time, Lapize was feeling a little less isolated since he had caught Vanhouwaert, as well as Garrigou, who had had a bad start and was coming from the back of beyond. And then it was Cruppelandt's turn to fall off the back of Faber's group, which was thus reduced to five.

So then what? Well, 54 kilometres from the Parc des Princes, something rather improbable happened: after 4,420 kilometres of madness, the Tour de France turned into an exercise in mental arithmetic. If Faber won the stage and Lapize came only seventh, a possible if not probable scenario, the two men would draw, with the same total of 64 points!

As if to ensure complete fairness, fate decreed that Faber should have his puncture, as Lapize had done at the start. At Saint-Nom-la-Brèche, Faber saw his tyre 'give up the ghost'. In spite of all his legendary energy, he could not catch the three riders ahead of him (Bettini had already been left). On the rain-soaked concrete of the Parc des Princes, Azzini outmuscled Ernest Paul and Ménager. Faber came in fourth and Bettini fifth.

Octave Lapize rallied the last of his strength to win his group's sprint and finish sixth. He had only dropped two points. The duel was over, and he had won by 63 points to 67.

Applause, bouquets, embraces. The *Marseillaise*...

Curtain.

* * * * *

Having diplomatically expressed his satisfaction at having won while avoiding any hint of triumphalism, and paid homage to the glorious runner-up, Octave Lapize, now offstage, let himself go. To his mother and his father he could only repeat 'I'm dead, dead! I can't go on.'

The public knew nothing of this. Everywhere, emotions were running high. Except, that is, beneath the pen of Henri Desgrange. This lying witness, who had not even seen the Tourmalet, allowed himself 'Some Reflections' in his paper on the Monday morning. It turned out that 'Mr Head and Legs' had no heart.* He wrote:

> There could be many reasons for me to take pleasure in the success of this eighth Tour de France, but first of all there is a fact we must face: we brought far too many people to Paris, and there was not enough wastage. This year, no serious fraud was possible among the latecomers and the disadvantaged; there was not a single one who did not cover the whole course. So, out of 110 starters, 41 riders finished the race. I repeat that this is far too many. The Tour de France has a reputation for being an extremely tough event; let us justify public opinion by putting new obstacles in front of our men. Fewer will make it through to Paris.

Monsieur Desgrange really was the only person to express such regrets. In the newspapers, and particularly *L'Auto*, the same word features in all the headlines: Apotheosis.

More objective analysis allows us to state with confidence that the 1910 Tour was indeed the greatest of the eight that had been held to date:

1. It had been the most hair-raising, the most open and at the same time the one with the most gruelling course. Lapize and Faber had put on a superb show. In 15 stages, they had only finished with the same time on a single occasion. That was in Roubaix, on the first day.

2. It had been the most closely followed and the most commented upon. The organisers saluted their colleagues in the provincial press who had given space to the event. There were around 20 of these. *La Petite Gironde* came in for particular

---

* *The Head and the Legs*, a book of advice and recommendations written by Henri Desgrange in 1894, had long been a reference in the cycling world. Today, it is almost unreadable. Nonetheless, its title has rightly passed into posterity.

praise for its special free edition distributed on the eve of the Luchon-Bayonne stage.

3. From the very first stages, the quality of the competitors had been judged significantly higher than in previous years. Very few riders had abandoned early on. The organisers had strengthened the race's reliability considerably with the invention of the broom wagon: the riders at the rear were controlled just as rigorously as those at the front. The race had stepped up a level.

4. For the first time, the average speed of the 1910 Tour had exceeded 29 kph. To be precise, it was 29.21 kph, an average that would not be beaten for another 25 years (in 1933, Speicher won with an average of 29.82 kph). The bicycle industry had contributed to this progress, with the improvements in pneumatic tyres and the invention of the freewheel, which was adopted by all riders from then on. In his column for *La Vie au Grand Air*, the sensible Petit-Breton emphasized 'the benefits of the freewheel, which I stubbornly resisted for so long, all because I neglected to try out this precious innovation.'

5. Octave Lapize was a superb winner, an absolute winner. He was first by any measure: in the general classification, the number of stage wins (four) and – had it existed – the King of the Mountains. He would also have won on the overall time. The sum of his times for the stages give him a lead of 52 minutes over Faber's total. He received all the trophies on offer, from that of *La Vie au Grand Air* to the one from *Political and Literary Annals*.

He also received a good deal of money. To the organisers' 7,525-franc prize must be added the bonuses from Alcyon (2,000 francs), Dunlop (4,000 francs) and countless special prizes given out along the entire length of the course. A reasonable estimate puts his total winnings at around 20,000 francs.

And it is to money that we are about to turn our thoughts.

* * * * *

After spending several days in his slippers, unable to wear his cycling shoes, Octave reappeared on the track. His velodrome training and his ability to accelerate made him a brilliant exponent of the discipline.

While the spectators were cheering the racers on, there was much disquiet at cycling's headquarters. It was customary to renew or to set up cyclist's contracts with their teams in the month of September. In other words, negotiations would begin shortly after the conclusion of the Tour de France. It is surprising, then, to note the position of François Faber, especially given his reputation for *bonhomie*. In his official and polite post-Tour interview, the Luxembourger said of Lapize that, 'The 1910 Tour was his, and I do not deny that he deserved it. However, it does not mean that I think I was beaten fair and square. I attribute it, which is my prerogative, to my fall in Bordeaux-Nantes. And I will certainly have my revenge!'

These measured terms actually masked a deep sense of bitterness. Several days later, Faber gave Messieurs Baugé and Calais to understand quite clearly that they would have to choose between him and Octave Lapize. Take it or leave it.

Lapize showed surprising discretion. With hindsight, one wonders whether he might not already have had an offer from the La Française-Diamant team in August. This manufacturer was also well established, on the Avenue de la Grande-Armée. It had renewed its involvement with road racing at the beginning of the year, but with a modesty that made it pine for the great successes of its huge star Maurice Garin, winner of Paris-Brest-Paris in 1901 and the 1903 Tour de France. True, La Française had picked the best little number on the track with Friol, French and world sprint champion, but its directors had never stopped dreaming of success on the road. It had not gone unnoticed that immediately after the finish of Paris–Roubaix in 1909, Messieurs Thiriot and Delattre of La Française had paid a visit to *L'Auto* in order to present the young victor with a gold medal. The paper added this comment: 'Is this not a fine sporting gesture; could there be a more fitting way to recognize the worth of a champion?'

Perhaps this medal had been the prelude to more extensive contacts which had led Lapize to look beyond Alcyon. On Sunday 25 September, Octave was the great favourite for Paris–Tours. Arriving to sign in at the Parc des Princes, he cast an eye over the list of entrants. To his amazement, he noted that Baugé had not entered either Garrigou or Vanhouwaert, his most valued team-mates. He did not let any indelicate expressions pass his lips, but suddenly declared himself to be unwell. He did not sign the register and instead went home to Villiers.

Later, on 6 November, he appeared at the Tour of Lombardy, but abandoned the race. In fact, he had decided to turn the page. Only just 23, Octave knew what he wanted, now that he knew what he was worth.

Lapize was in vigorous discussions with Monsieur Hammond, the boss of La Française. It is even possible to imagine that, for the first time in French cycling history, a new kind of contract was being drawn up: one that dealt with both the short and the medium term. Octave Lapize was no ordinary rider. It was at this moment that Charles Ravaud, the journalist but also a close witness, wrote:

> Lapize is 23 years of age, but with the head of a man twice his age. I understand very well why Desgrange cannot stop singing his praises and why Messieurs Hammond and Mouter have put him on a pedestal. Lapize has both head and legs, a rare combination in cycling champions. Lapize knows how to negotiate his interests as well as how to negotiate a bend in the track.

With the hint of a reproach, Charles Ravaud adds that 'Lapize is perhaps too much of a businessman.'

The famous contract between Lapize and La Française would make a great impression on the followers of sport. At great cost, and with his agreement, Monsieur Hammond had built a line-up around Lapize that was capable of threatening the hegemony of the Alcyon team. He had signed Petit-Breton, who needs no introduction, and Cruchon, who had won the *isolé* category in the Tour de France. No doubt for the classic races, he had also recruited the Roubaix man, Cruppelandt and the Belgian Vanhouwaert. Above all, he had retained the services of Émile Georget, the reigning French champion, not an insignificant factor, because La Française's Diamant machines were 'black with the tricolour head badge'. The valiant Charpiot and Lorgeau completed the line-up.

What escaped the attention of the sporting public was the other side – the business section – of the famous contract. Fifty years later, Eugène Christophe told me, 'I knew nothing about it, but I think it was quite a coup!' Quite simply, Lapize had given the rights to his name to the brand that would race him. For an unknown period, but which I estimate at 10 years (following my research at the National Institute for Industrial Property), La Française would produce and sell bicycles and accessories in the champion's name. Last but not least, Octave found himself the manager of a large shop bearing his name at 112, Boulevard de la Chapelle.

By the beginning of 1911, Lapize the racer would have increased his social status considerably. This is the moment to let you into a secret. The cagey Octave was also making considerable adjustments to his private life. He left his mum and dad in Villiers-dur-Marne for an apartment at 11, rue Ambroise-Paré in Paris's 10th *arrondissement*. And he was not alone. Why? It is a lovely story, even if I do not know the exact details. Octave Lapize was now sharing his life with Juliette Peyrot: the pretty girl, you might remember, whom he never forgot to invite for a ride with the fine team from his father's brasserie. They were not married, and never would be. Their love for each other provoked only one question in the family. However had they managed to find each other again? We will have to think up our own answer, because we shall never know.

Octave at seventeen.

Arrivée de Lapize au sommet du Tourmalet, le 21 Juillet 1910 (7h ½ mat.)

1910. The first Tourmalet in Tour de France history.

1910 Tour. On the rest day in Caen, Lapize discovers flying.

1910 Tour. At last, the finish in Paris,
after a 250-kilometre pursuit in the rain.

1910 Tour. Octave is welcomed at the Parc des Princes
by his mother.

Champion of France
in 1911,1912 and 1913.

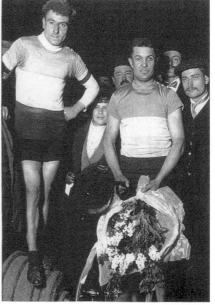

January 1913. Lapize (left)
and Dupré win the Paris
Six-Hours at the Vel' d'Hiv.

1916. Drill Sergeant Lapize.

1917. Lapize's second plane. N90 planes were emblazoned with
the silhouette of a 'crowing rooster in profile'.

The O. Lapize catalogue. The brand survived
the champion for many years.

PARIS – BREST – NEW YORK

In 1911, the return of La Française to competition seemed to increase Alcyon's appetite for winning – if that were still possible – and stimulate its battle plan. No expense was spared: Faber and his comrades had everything they wanted to prepare for the new season. They were living in some style. While training on the Côte d'Azur, the riders received a telegram announcing the arrival of a new boy, just recovering from depression following a bad experience of military service. His name was Henri Pélissier. He had hardly had time to put down his suitcases when big François, finding the Nice weather not quite nice enough, decided he would rather train in Algeria instead. That was all it took! The whole Alcyon team upped sticks and went to ride from Algiers to Tunis by way of Sousse and Bizerte, in eight 150-kilometre stages, with five kilograms of luggage. Then, on disembarking at Gênes, they returned to Paris in stages of 200 kilometres. The result was that the daily level of effort required by the colossus Faber was too much for the fragile Pélissier, who returned to Paris on his knees.

Lapize, meanwhile, stuck to his normal régime. Serious in his daily life, he kept up a steady 100 kilometres per day, more often than not on his own. He tried to get into his stride by taking part in track events such as the American-style Six Days.

Bizarrely, the start of the season was once again postponed until 2 April. I say bizarrely, because there was a choice that day between Milan–San Remo and Paris–Tours. Henri Desgrange, who believed he could do anything, had rescheduled his autumn race with the excuse that the contestants would be exhausted in September from Paris-Brest-Paris, which he held at the end of August. The consequence of this sleight of hand was that we would never know the comparative merits of this or that training method, because the Alcyon brand, attracted by the Italian market, entered its riders for Milan–San Remo.

Nonetheless, 77 riders started Paris–Tours. In the wind and rain, the peloton stayed intact as far as Blois where, thanks to the control point, things livened up a bit. In the throng, Vanhouwaert leapt from group to group like an acrobat to get his signature on the register and slip away on the quiet. But the equally cunning Lapize had spotted him. He rushed off in pursuit and caught him at the edge of town, and the double-act was off again at a fiendish pace. One witness recalled that the others were 'flabbergasted'. Not for long, mind, because Émile Georget, Pautrat, Charpiot and Verschore set off on their trail and closed the gap on the pair of escapees. They passed Amboise in the same formation, and the six rivals hit the track of the Tours velodrome in Indian file. Paris–Tours culminated in a speed contest in which Octave Lapize demonstrated his superiority. Vanhouwaert finished at half a length and Charpiot at one length. As the sun came out during the laps of honour, La Française savoured its clean sweep of the top three places.

In San Remo, meanwhile, it was Garrigou who was winning ahead of Trousselier, and there were seven Alcyon riders among the first 11 finishers. It didn't help. In the 3 April edition of *L'Auto*, Paris–Tours spread across three columns and two pages, while Milan–San Remo could only muster a single column on page five. It was time for round two.

The second round was Paris–Roubaix on 16 April. Sorry about the lack of suspense, but I have to tell you the outcome straight away because it was fantastic, unheard-of. Octave Lapize won his third Paris–Roubaix in the most convincing way possible, finishing alone with a lead of four minutes.

His team had cleaned up on the climb at Doullens. At the crest, Lapize was in the lead with Vanhouwaert and Charpiot again, and a Belgian rider who had managed to latch on:

Vandenberghe from the Armor team. It was Charpiot who dedicated himself to keeping up the pace so as to prevent the possible return of the Alcyon riders, who had completely missed the boat. Charpiot passed the baton 20 kilometres from the finish and a little further on Vanhouwaert punctured. Lapize, with impressive ease, gave a masterclass. At the finish, they had to wait three minutes and 50 seconds to see Charpiot arrive, and another minute for Vanhouwaert. It was a nice triple win for La Française, but a superb hat-trick for Lapize, who did not hide his delight. He was very happy to prove himself to those who had called him a lucky rider, and to win in the sprint, even though he was the only one there. 'It doesn't matter. I'd have given anything to win three in a row like that. It's a real feat. And I would very much like to do it again.' Did he imagine that his triple in the Paris–Roubaix was just the beginning?

The season's third round came on 20 April, in the highly offical form of the French Championship, organised along the traditional course: Versailles-Ablis-Rambouillet-Dampierre-Versailles. Brimming with confidence, Octave carried on with his pageant. He won, alone once again, a minute ahead of Garrigou. Monsieur Hammond, the manufacturer of bicycles 'with tricolour head badge' was overjoyed at this victory. There was one small incident at the finish in Versailles. The ceremony where the champion's tricolour jersey would be presented was held at the Parc des Princes velodrome. Octave decided to go by car, but the finicky French Cycling Union officials insisted that he, like all the other competitors, get to the Parc des Princes 'by the means of locomotion that has brought him victory.' You didn't mess about with the regulations.

From that day forth – 30 April 1911 – Octave Lapize would never again be seen in the famous blue jersey with the claret trim of his club, the Paris Cyclists' Union. He had just taken out a long lease on the blue, white and red jersey.

Wearing the national colours, the champion provoked many questions and covetous looks, echoed in *La Vie au Grand Air*.

'This likeable rider is scooping all the prizes and his rivals are beginning to ask themselves what the mysterious secret of his success can be, which he achieves with such virtuosity. Quality has a large part to play in success, but it must be said that good fortune has helped as well.'

François Faber was one of the most impatient and was simmering away, plotting his revenge in Bordeaux–Paris on 13-14 May. There were 52 at the start, and everyone was thinking big. Alcyon did not prevent Faber from using the outrageous 78-inch gear, even though everybody else was going for 70 to 73 inches. La Française, hungry for another victory, promised its champion a special bonus of 5,000 francs.

But it was Faber who won, at an average of almost 32 kph, gaining himself a substantial reward from his backers, of the same order as the one promised to Lapize, who was roundly beaten: he had abandoned on the banks of the Loire.

There was no time to get bored. The classic for the month of June was Paris–Brussels, and all the champions had entered. The reporters were rubbing their hands at the idea of a Lapize vs. Faber match and another clash between La Française and Alcyon. The French champion was doubly 'motivated', as we would say nowadays, since the starting line was drawn in Villers-sur-Marne, and because this time he was keen to win 'good and proper'. He had not forgotten his relegation of the previous year.

The race was marked at the outset by a *coup de théâtre*. They had not gone 10 kilometres when Faber punctured. He lost a good deal of time over the incident, while 20 riders broke away, maintaining a strong pace. Faber was left seven minutes behind, then ten. He had almost been forgotten when suddenly he reappeared at the front at Rocroi after a gargantuan – 'Faberian' – chase that had lasted 250 kilometres. The pace had dropped as everybody regained their breath. At the French/ Belgian border, Lapize, who had stopped for a moment, went back up the line to his place. On the way, he drew alongside the car in which M. Gentil was sitting, pleased as Punch to have witnessed Faber's return. And Lapize allowed himself a little bit of banter.

'You're going to regret letting me go.'

'Oh, yes? Why is that, then?' retorted M. Gentil.

'Because I'm about to win Paris–Brussels!'

And so he did. Eight riders hit the Linthout velodrome together. Lapize outsprinted Faber by the narrowest of margins: a quarter of a wheel! Mid-season, Octave already had a hatful of victories: he was champion of France, and had won three classics.

But forget about the classics: it was already Tour de France time, about to leave on 2 July, and to set a new altitude record with the 2,556m climb up the Col du Galibier. The talk was not so much of the Galibier, though, as about revenge and resumption of the famous duel of 1910. The race got off to an extremely strong start from the very first stage from Paris to Dunkerque. Mid-way, a figure in a tricolour jersey was seen to stop on the verge to repair a burst tyre. There was much commotion and confusion in the caravan because many people did not recognize Lapize without his moustache: he had shaved it off a short time before. As soon as the news was confirmed that it was indeed the French champion on his rims, the other riders could not resist thinking and even shouting out loud: 'At last! We've been waiting a year for this moment.' In Dunkerque, Octave could only manage 11th place. But that was not the real problem.

The truth was that Lapize was not up to taking part in this Tour. He had expended too much energy since the beginning of the year. He ought to have paced himself, building in some rest periods from time to time. I know that this did not happen. In my hands, which are trembling slightly with emotion, I am holding his personal diary, marked 'Town Hall Bazaar. 1911.' In this little brown notebook, he has made a note of all the track racing contracts he fulfilled after Paris–Roubaix, detailing for each one the venue and the fee. In April, he raced twice behind tandems in Buffalo. On 7 May he was in Geneva, on the fine concrete track at La Jonction. In Belgium, where the pay was highest, he turned out at Ghent, Charleroi and Evergem. His tour did not even let up in June, when on top of his official programme of demanding events, he contested another 12 track races! With an average of 500 francs per race plus prize money, he had built up a nice little nest egg. And plenty of fatigue.

Lapize was in trouble from the second stage of the Tour, to Longwy, and on the Ballon d'Alsace between Longwy and Belfort he could not keep up with the leaders. His abandonment during the fourth, Belfort-Chamonix, stage was announced by a telegram from Morez-du-Jura:

> There has been a major incident here: Lapize, who had been among the favourites for the 1911 Tour, has abandoned. The French champion could not go on. Feeling in poor shape, and – truth to tell – very tired from taking part in too many races since the start of the season, he has decided to drop out. All the exhortations and pleas have been in vain: the great ace would hear none of them.

The Tour de France went on without him – and without François Faber, who fell victim to food poisoning shortly afterwards. Garrigou, a most consistent rider (he would finish six Tours in the top three) was the ultimate victor. The race went down in history because of a scandal that was nothing short of an attempted poisoning. In the Pyrenean stages, a rider named Duboc from the La Française team was clear of the bunch and with a chance of claiming top spot in the general classification. Shortly after the feeding station at Argèles-Gazost, he collapsed on the road after drinking the contents of a bottle. There was no doubt that it was a poisoning (the criminal hand behind it would only be revealed much later). There was no doubt, either, at the time, that the unfortunate Duboc was suddenly saved by vomiting. In fact, Duboc was put back in the saddle – secretly, because it was against the rules – by his new *directeur sportif* who had managed to give him some strong medicine. Under the leadership of this new *directeur*, who had arrived after Lapize's departure, the La Française team would win five stage victories. The name of the miracle-worker was Paul Ruinart whose name, the following year, would become synonymous with the Vélo-Club de Levallois, the most prestigious amateur club of all time.

But let us get back to the business in hand.

Octave Lapize had realized his mistake, and took July off altogether to rest. He spent the better part of August in Belgium, where he rode in five track events until the 20th of the month. Why stop there, you might ask? Because 25 to 27 August was reserved for the third edition of the decennial Paris-Brest-Paris. And Lapize had decided to take part, no doubt because of all the legends surrounding this unique event. Since 1901, *L'Auto* had been the organiser of this race, invented in 1891 by Pierre Giffard of the *Petit Journal*, and Desgrange described it in these terms:

> We have given this race a special mark of respect by holding it only every ten years, in order to preserve the unique character which sets it apart from all the other road events, with which it has nothing in common.

In 1901, La Française had triumphed with Maurice Garin, but the team had never asked Lapize to go in for a 1,200-kilometre event, which was considered too long for him – and after Bordeaux–Paris – but the stubborn Lapize insisted on taking part. The no less pigheaded Faber was also signed up. Both riders, no doubt, were thinking that 1921 would be too late.

On Friday 25 August, it seemed that the whole of Paris was on the streets to see off the 102 contenders, who were divided into two categories: 13 'fast riders' (the equivalent of team riders in the Tour de France) and 89 'tourists' (the *isolés*). A procession had been organised from Montmartre to the Pont de Suresnes, passing by the Grand Boulevards, the Place de la

Concorde, the Champs-Elysées, the Arc de Triomphe and the Porte Dauphine. Two hundred policemen were unable to hold back the surges of a delirious crowd. Nonetheless, the start was given as planned at 12:30pm. Maurice Brocco, wasting no time, sped off on his own. Nobody panicked. Leading by up to 11 minutes at Dreux, Brocco realized that this was madness: he was caught, then dropped towards Mortagne. This was where it was noticed that Faber was not in lively form. He had caught a cold, it was rumoured, and the only reason he was able to keep up was that the headwind was slowing the pace. The impatient followers at Morlaix (526 kilometres) noted that the leading group of 10 tightly bunched riders was an hour and a half behind the anticipated schedule.

On reaching Brest (598 kilometres), Faber dropped out. Six riders arrived together at the halfway control point: Cornet, Vanhouwaert, Ernest Paul, Émile Georget, Cruchon and Lapize. It was one o'clock on the Saturday afternoon. The escapees had been in the saddle for 25 hours and thirteen minutes. The reporters, becoming ever more morose, noted that a decade earlier, the same distance had been covered in a time three hours shorter. However, with a following wind now, there was a noticeable quickening of the pace. It was kept regular by the four La Française riders in the leaders' group, taking turns to pull at the front. Georget, Lapize, Vanhouwaert and Cruchon were not really trying to get rid of Cornet and Ernest Paul who, for their part, were hanging on to their apron strings because they had no desire to ride alone through the second night, which was about to fall.

Before Rennes, Lapize suffered a brief spell of weakness. At the control point there (845 kilometres), it was 18 minutes to one in the morning when Vanhouwaert and Georget signed the register and left, or rather escaped without waiting for the others. Lapize, in a bad way, was talking about abandoning the race. His *soigneurs* cheered him up again and he set off alone into the night. At the front, Vanhouwaert and Cornet were making mincemeat out of each other under the amused gaze of Georget, mounting murderous attacks and slowing down unpredictably by turns – and Lapize was back among the leaders. It was not until Alençon, where they clocked in at 7:32am, that the five trailblazers could be seen in the light of day. Georget was certainly in the best shape. Vanhouwaert was having such trouble keeping his eyes open that his bike was zigzagging across the road. Lapize and Cornet, after their accordion-like trajectory – being dropped, coming back, hanging on – were visibly tiring. Ernest Paul was the most enigmatic. By agreement, the five of them took a few minutes out to let the *soigneurs* give them a proper wash and brush-up. They shed their thick woollen pullovers and slipped into lighter jerseys, a wise move since the sun was coming into play. It soon overcame Vanhouwaert, who was struggling against the combined forces of sleep and sun. The Belgian was dropped for good. Cornet met the same fate at Mortagne, 150 kilometres from the finish.

The decisive moment came on the climb at Nonancourt. Georget took off at the very moment Lapize cracked for the second time. There was no question of abandoning this time, however, and at Dreux (1,116 kilometres), the French champion asked his *soigneurs* for a long massage. He did not mind waiting a bit longer, and even let Ernest Paul through into second place. Neither of them would see Georget again that day. But Lapize, perked up again, caught and passed Ernest Paul. It was 2:44pm on that Sunday 27 August when Émile Georget crossed the finishing line at the Parc des Princes, with a time of 50 hours, fourteen minutes and 24 seconds. He beat the previous record by around two hours, but the distinguishing feature of the performance was that, for the first time, the average speed on the return leg was higher than that of the outward journey: 23.9, against 23.7 kph. Lapize surprised everybody by grabbing second place (at 20 minutes) in an event hardly designed with a refined racer like him in mind. He was not altogether dissatisfied with his achievement.

As always with Paris-Brest, there were sizeable gaps between the riders. The last rider in the 'fast' category, the

Belgian Lambot, finished ninth, more than a day after the victor – 26 hours and eleven minutes, to be precise. However, the nicest story is that of the last 'tourist'. His name was Vogt, and he arrived in Paris – six days after Georget. This Vogt was a gentleman, however. Passing through the village of Javron on the return leg, he insisted on attending the funeral of one of his comrades, Rubeaux, who had been killed hurtling downhill in the dark. Henri Desgrange had been right to say that Paris-Brest-Paris was a race unlike any other.

Octave soon put the exertions of this fantastical epic ride behind him, and quickly got back down to the serious business of racing for hard cash, above all in Belgium. Three days after Paris-Brest-Paris, the little diary from the Town Hall Bazaar reports that he was in Leuven (a 600-franc contract, plus prizes). He made further appearances in Liège, Brussels, Erqueline, Boom – around 10 meetings, all told, until 10 October. After all, he had to while away the time somehow while waiting for the start of the last classic of the season on 5 November: the Tour of Lombardy. In fine fettle at the start in Milan, Lapize began the scrap alongside the Italians Ganna and Pavesi: a puncture left him briefly on the side of the road before he resumed his place in the peloton. Unfortunately, he was involved in a fall with Rossignoli on the way through Varese, and was forced to pull out.

Phew! The season was over, and what a season it had been for the French champion. For all the chroniclers, 1911 was the Year of Lapize. As they usually say in such circumstances, it was time for a well- earned rest.

And this is where we will take a short break, ourselves.

* * * * *

We will leave Lapize the champion in 1911 for a while, and have a chat with his daughter Yvonne in 2002. I am asking her about a time three years before her birth in 1914 and, quite frankly, the victories of the father do not inspire very much admiration in his daughter. I sugar the pill a little by mentioning that Octave was also a very accomplished track racer. She agrees because, 'as Mum used to say, we lived near the Gare du Nord, so it was easy to get to Belgium.' I step into the breach between memories to risk a tentative enquiry: 'Did you know that some people claim that he went not only to Belgium, but also as far as America?'

Yvonne Lapize sits up, a twinkle in her eye. 'America? Of course he went to America, to race in a championship or something like that in New York.' Any lingering doubts I had were quickly swept away as the details of the story, which had obviously been told to Yvonne by her mother Juliette and filed among the deepest and most amusing family memories, unfolded before me.

'Listen, Dad must have been tired out after the journey and from his championship. He was so tired that when he came back to the house, or rather to our apartment block, he came up to the wrong floor. He stopped at the first landing, where the door to the apartment and its handle were the same as ours on the floor above. He went in, noticed that something had changed, but just thought 'Ah, Juliette has moved the furniture around' and slumped onto a sofa. That's when the lady on the first floor came out of her kitchen and saw him. She knew him fairly well, but it was still quite a surprise.' A little time went by and Yvonne Lapize concluded: 'Ah yes, he went to America all right, and America did him in.'

It's hardly surprising.

At five minutes to midnight on Sunday 12 December 1911, in Madison Square Gardens, New York, everyone was in position for the presentation of the contestants in the Six Days. In contrast to all the excitement only moments before, silence fell over the vélodrome. First, the European teams rode out for a lap of the

160-metre track. Lapize, Brocco, (Léon) Georget, Vanhouwaert, Lorenz and Saldow were given a rousing reception. Then it was the American teams' turn to arrive and the crowd went wild. Kramer had to make several laps of honour. Along with Moran, who was also given an earsplitting ovation, Kramer was without question the darling of this huge crowd. At five past midnight, the 15 teams took their places and the starter's pistol rang out. The great cycle ride was under way. It had had to wait until five past midnight – officially 00:05 on Monday morning in New York – for the event to be legal, because racing on a Sunday was not allowed.

This is how Octave Lapize came to be in New York, and not as the support act. His name topped the bill. His tricolour jersey bore the number 1, which he shared with his team-mate Vanhouwaert.

Riding into Madison Square, he had discovered the scenery of the race to come. On the turf, which was quite restricted because the track was only 160m long, tents had been put up where the Six Day Men had a chance to rest or to take some restorative drugs 'on the quiet'. On the boat, Léon Georget, who was seen as the old hand of the European delegation, had extolled the virtues of 'the skilful massages and the well concocted drugs.' Léon Georget had 'done' New York with his brother Émile in 1907, when he wrote:

> For the first few days, no stimulants. Towards the middle, one or two pick-me-ups, and on the last day, the entire range from alcohol to cafeine. Of course we didn't actually need to swallow a mixture or a glass of champagne every ten minutes, but it seems to be standard practice.

Sitting amid the roar in the stalls, Octave had a good view of all the characters invading the pitch below: the *soigneurs*, the officials, the VIPs and the sporting enthusiasts rich enough to be able to afford to follow the race from the inside. What organisation!

The only way to understand this race was to do it. In this strange new world, and this foreign arena, the American racers were past masters. Charles Ravaud, waiting feverishly in his office at *L'Auto* for the next cable from New York, took his courage in his hands to hazard a prediction:

> First of all, I am going quite dispassionately to strike out the three European teams from the list. Lapize is not a rider to last out six days in the saddle and Vanhouwaert lacks speed. Brocco and Léon Georget will fare better, but the brave Léon will be snuffed out by some trickery. As for the German pair, their victory in Mainz is hardly an adequate qualification.

Indeed, you had to have done this race before. For the first hours, and even the first two days of the race, the Europeans held on and put up a decent show. Later on, when the Americans stepped on the gas, things took a turn for the worse and they could no longer hope for anything more than to keep going bravely until the end. Working from the final cable from New York, Charles Ravaud described:

> The classic Six Day race at Madison Square Gardens has ended in victory for the fearsome Clark-Fogler team. Their success will come as no surprise, since both have won before with other partners. But this year the Australian (Clark) and Fogler have outdone everybody. By dominating the favourites, Kramer and Moran, they have proven themselves both extremely brave riders and complete athletes. Although they did not break the record, they came within 100 kilometres of it, covering a distance of 4,375 kilometres and 544 metres. The Europeans failed to shine, except for the Germans who finished seventh, one lap behind the winners. Georget and Brocco, Lapize and Vanhouwaert did what they could, but the coalition lined up against them was a formidable one. They

had to contend with the fatigue of their voyage as well as the demands of a six-day race.

For his part, Lapize proved once and for all that he has remarkable staying power. In the final classification, Brocco-Georget were placed eighth, 13 laps off the lead, and Lapize-Vanhouwaert ninth, at 15 laps.

This baptism of fire in six-day racing was a harsh one, and we can better understand why, on his return to 11, rue Ambrois-Paré, Octave Lapize went to the wrong floor and collapsed on the first sofa he found.

A TENSE ATMOSPHERE

The new year brought a change of continents, but Lapize's racing life hardly altered at all. New York was still topical. Numerous American racers had crossed the Atlantic with him, drawn by the lucrative European programme of events. Did someone say lucrative? In Paris, Octave would learn a thing or two about New York. To be sure, he had earned enough money on the other side of the pond to guarantee himself a fixed contract, duly signed and sealed. But the Americans Clark and Fogler had negotiated themselves a better deal by agreeing to take part for a percentage of the gates. The Six Days had been such a success that each had pocketed the equivalent of 8,500 francs (by way of comparison, Garrigou had earned only 5,000 francs for winning the Tour de France). Such revelations put Monsieur Durand, the Director of the Vélodrome d'Hiver, on his guard. Of course, he went ahead and invited the American champions, but he rejected their ways of doing things, and even their rules. When the press announced with a great fanfare that the Paris Six Hours would be 'just like Madison Square,' they were mistaken. The Paris organisers turned a deaf ear to the grievances of the American champions, who complained about the European riders' untimely accelerations in New York. Paris had established a stricter set of rules and intended to see them respected. On 19 February 1912, the Paris Six Hours brought together 18 teams, of which three were American, seen as the great favourites, and a good number of French teams which were nonetheless given some credit. It is worth mentioning that invitations had gone out to road riders such as Garrigou, Georget and, of course, Lapize. Henri Desgrange was showing great interest in what promised to be 'as much a battle of intelligence as brawn.' For him, in a race like this, 'it is just as dangerous for the brain to tire as for the legs.'

At 10:30am on that Sunday morning, the start was given in front of a packed and excited auditorium. By 4:30pm the winners had covered 234.3 kilometres at the end of an unrelenting scrap. The crowd was over the moon, because these winners were Octave Lapize and Émile Georget. At the end of the fifth hour, 'when the superb Lapize suddenly attacked,' the French team had gone a lap ahead, and held off all assaults for the last 60 minutes. The Americans Fogler-Moran were runners-up, beating the seven other teams in the same lap in the final sprint. The *Marseillaise* rang out as the champions in blue, white and red took their lap of honour. *L'Auto* did not fail to underline the victory of the leading brands La Française and Dunlop. There was just one question on everybody's lips: when would they see a Paris Six Days?

A little more patience would be needed. For the time being, Octave Lapize had to put the smoke and fury of the velodrome out of his head.

On the road, on his return from America, Octave Lapize found the French cycling landscape had changed noticeably. There had been some important developments while he was away. Although the formation of a new team, Automoto, was not such a surprise, the name of its leader must have been a real bombshell: it was Faber! Faber had parted company with his friend Baugé and with Alcyon. Even the celebrations to mark the transfer were on a 'Faberian' scale: a three-day party in Colombes with about 30 friends. What a man!

But Alcyon was far from surrendering. Baugé, who soon won a reputation as the man who made or unmade teams and riders, kept his faith in Garrigou, around whom there had been a whiff of treachery in 1910, and took on Duboc, the victim of a murky assassination attempt in the 1911 Tour. Since he also had half an eye on the Flemish market, which was looking more and more promising, he signed up the reigning Belgian champion, one Odile Defraye. Alcyon even played a double game, introducing a subsidiary team, Thomann, into the peloton under its leader, the young Henri Pélissier.

Mood music...

Another development of a different kind caused much ink to flow. Victor Breyer left *L'Auto* and went over to join *L'Écho des Sports* as Chairman of its Board of Directors. *L'Écho* marked the new signing with a warm editorial under the headline 'At Last!' Victor Breyer was said to want to rebalance the content of his newspaper, best known for its gossip and merciless satire, with more rigorous news reporting. In those days, the competition between cycle brands and the quarrels between rival newspapers were particularly bitter. This was thanks to the importance of advertising and, more specifically, of the supplements ordered and paid for by the manufacturers. It is hardly an exaggeration to say that the cycling industry provided the sporting press with the bulk of its resources. In *L'Auto*, the number of pages given to advertising sometimes exceeded that accorded to news. Its competitors, less well-endowed, denounced this excess, which was bound to lead to a loss of objectivity. One day, Victor Breyer got angry: 'We also have Automoto and Alcyon amongst our clients and we welcome advertisements, too.' But *L'Écho des Sports* aimed to keep a critical distance and Breyer intended to show the rest (of whom could I be thinking?) that, 'a group of decent people can create, through honesty and perseverance alone, an honest product.'

Mood music...

The tyre companies were the most generous. Dunlop and Hutchinson had to deal with the threat of ambitious smaller manufacturers such as Persan, Russian or Soly. What about Michelin, you might ask? Well, Michelin had withdrawn from cycling, which it had so pampered during its infancy in the era of Charles Terront and the first Paris-Brest-Paris (1891).

Michelin pulled out at great expense and in a blaze of publicity, paying for an entire page in order to address a short message to its clients and suppliers: 'Michelin is taking no further part in racing.'

More mood music…

The time for racing came round again. Paris–Tours opened the season on 24 March, a week before Milan–San Remo and a fortnight before Paris–Roubaix. That spring was not an auspicious one for Lapize. It is not that he was slackening. Although, like Petit-Breton, he had bought himself a car, it was clear to all the observers that nothing had changed in either his training régime or his lifestyle. It is just that he was lacking that extra impetus that comes with being in one's best form, and experiencing that slight hinderance that comes with not winning.

The outcome of Paris–Tours was decided by the wind and rain, which Lapize did not like, and by Faber, of whom Lapize was wary. Fifteen kilometres from the finish, there were only seven men at the front. But what men! They included an unbridled Faber, Petit-Breton, Émile Georget and Lapize: the winners, between them, of four Tours de France, four Paris–Tours, three Paris–Roubaix, one Paris-Brest-Paris, one Paris-San Remo and one Tour of Lombardy. These four aces were accompanied by three Belgians with a lower profile: Heusghem, Blaise and Deruyter. Strangely enough, following some poorly controlled attacks, it was Heusghem who won on the track in Tours. Lapize, who had been lying third at the edge of town, gave up, vexed, and did not even cross the threshold of the velodrome.

He took no part in Milan–San Remo: Italy brought him bad luck. It seemed to favour Pélissier, though, who added the 1912 Milan–San Remo to his Tour of Lombardy victory of 1911. One small detail: in San Remo, Pélissier was not riding for Thomann, but Alcyon.

In Paris–Roubaix, Octave would hear the same tune as in Paris–Tours. At Séclin, 20 kilometres from the finish, there were (again!) seven riders in the lead. Which of them could hope to outsprint Lapize in 'his' race, people wondered. But, in the final kilometres, the attacks came thick and fast, gaps opened up, and three riders made a break for it. They were not caught, and the winner was Cruppelandt. 250 metres behind, Lapize took fourth place. His disappointment was (slightly) tempered since Cruppelandt was a team-mate at La Française. But still, Octave had dreamed of winning a fourth Paris–Roubaix.

He made up for it in the French 100-kilometre championship in Versailles, which he won with ease and kept hold of his tricolour jersey, much to the satisfaction of his aptly-named employer, La Française.

At this point in the season, the end of May, he made the mistake of entering Bordeaux–Paris. It was no use telling him that this race did not suit him: he stuck to his guns, retorting that if he could make second place in Paris-Brest-Paris, he could come first in Bordeaux–Paris. He was wrong: as in the previous year, he abandoned before Orléans.

If he was to avoid losing everything, Octave had to make a comeback in the last race before the Tour: Paris–Brussels.

In order to make sure, Octave did something entirely out of character and entered himself for a second-rank race. Following Octave around the elite circuit of the great international competitions, we could easily forget that the French cycling calendar was teeming with other events, most of which took place in the provinces.

On Sunday 2 June, presumably to the delight of its organisers, the Circuit de Touraine was won by Octave Lapize, who outsprinted the Belgians Van Daele and Spiessens at the end of a 260-kilometre course. Now he was in the right frame of mind to confront the 425 kilometres of Paris–Brussels.

On the roads of the North, Lapize was very much in his element, and he was riding in a group of nine riders without apparent effort as they approached the finish. Effortless, perhaps, but not without some anxiety. With no team-mate in sight, he was surrounded by five Peugeot and three Alcyon riders. But this time, luck was on his side. He narrowly avoided a fall caused by a gendarme and won his second Paris–Brussels in the sprint. Why not go for a hat trick next year? Well, because there was more room for doubt these days, given the number of emerging new talents coming into the peloton. Behind Lapize, a veteran at 24 years old, the runner-up, Luguet, had just turned 20 and the third-placed rider, the Swiss Oscar Egg, was 21. Three months later, this Oscar Egg was to set an amazing hour record by covering a distance of 42.36 kilometres. This simply goes to show that, in 1912, they could already go pretty fast on a bicycle.

But us get back to the main road, because the Tour de France is coming.

* * * * *

The 1912 Tour flaunted what would henceforth become its customary challenges: more than 5,000 kilometres divided across 15 stages, the Alps with the Galibier, the Pyrenees with the Tourmalet and a gargantuan stage of 470 kilometres from La Rochelle to Brest. In order to embellish the décor in Paris, the organisers carried out the registration in the Salle des Phénomènes and the *Grand Départ* took place amongst the splendid attractions of the Luna Park.

Eighty independents or *isolés* had been accepted for the Tour, alongside 50 *groupés* or team riders. There were many favourites. La Française was pinning its hopes on Lapize, Alcyon on Garrigou, Peugeot on Petit-Breton, Automoto on Faber, Armor on Christophe. Although the other teams were less well-endowed with champions, their sheer number bore witness to the vitality of the bicycle industry. Their names were Griffon, Le Globe, J-B Louvet and Thomann. For the first time there were now almost as many Belgians as Frenchmen in the *groupés* category. Only the La Française team, appropriately, was 100% French.

The race unfolded without incident as far Grenoble, bringing two unexpected names to the fore. Eugène Christophe won three stages in succession: in Belfort, Chamonix and Grenoble. But it was the winner of the second stage in Longwy, Alcyon's Belgian rider, Defraye, who was leading in the general classification. His lead, however, was very insecure since the second-placed Christophe had the same number of points, and Lapize, lying in third, was just one point behind. Having kept such a low profile in the initial stages that he almost disappeared from view, Octave suddenly came to life on the Galibier, where he rode magnificently to come in 'a good second' in Grenoble. His followers were delighted to see that he had lost none of his abilities.

The sixth stage from Grenoble to Nice gave the French champion his opportunity to confirm himself as the favourite. From the climb at Laffrey onward, he set a brisk pace, keeping up the pursuit of the escapee Alavoine, and at Barcelonnette there were only six men left in the vanguard. And then there were three. Finally, only two remained, when Christophe dropped off the pace shortly after the control point. These two were Defray and Lapize, who hit the first slopes of the Col d'Allos together, still known locally as the Valjeleye or 'pretty valley'. Henri Desgrange himself fell under its spell:

> Over the 17-kilometre ascent from sea level to the permanent snowline, I had the impression that I was looking at two brothers, or at least two thoroughbred athletes. They say that a pair of fine boxers make for a fine boxing match; well-matched fencers provide a fine display of swordsmanship. They gave us a display of cycling at its best. To watch the ease and harmony of their pedalling was to feel a healthy and complete satisfaction. They rode a 'classic': it was literally perfect.

At the end of the race, Lapize's task was made easier by an unfortunate puncture for Defraye, who lost nine minutes, though only a single point, to the stage winner.

A whole edition of *L'Auto* was caught up in the eulogy. Its headline, 'Virtue is Always Rewarded', was followed by the subtitle 'The great ace from La Française, Diamant and Dunlop, goes to the top of the classification with Defraye.'

On the rest day in Nice, Lapize was able to take full benefit from the landscape and the sun on the *Promenade des Anglais*. But, in spite of the fine weather, metaphorical stormclouds gathered over the next stages between Nice and Marseille and Marseille-Perpignan. Lapize had absolutely no support from his team-mates who missed two clear opportunities to overhaul Defraye by a good 10 points. 'Is it because these riders are completely deaf to the advice they are being given? Or are they not being given the advice regularly enough?' Henri Desgrange was unstinting in his criticism of La Française and its manager Thiriot, insisting:

> It is lamentable that there should be so little understanding between riders of the same team when what is at stake is the winning or losing of an event of this importance. I continue to believe that a man as valuable as Lapize, who is without doubt and by far the finest of our French road riders, should find in his comrades the entire and full assistance that our rules allow.

This was a fine homage from the *patron* to the champion. Such was Lapize's prestige at this point that everyone was convinced that he would put on a rerun of his 1910 display in the Pyrenees, starting in Luchon and finishing in Bayonne. On Wednesday 17 July 1912, at 3:15am, a huge crowd gathered in Perpignan to see off the 63 riders still in the race. This date would reverberate in the annals of the Tour, and would be referred to many times. And here's why.

Christophe and the Belgian Buysse lost no time in launching their attack, even before the Col du Portet. In Quillan (75 kilometres), they posted a lead of five minutes over a group of about 30 riders led by Lapize, the better to keep an eye on Defraye. This situation hardly changed all the way to Saint-Girons (80 kilometres from the finish), where the party was in full swing. The two escapees had extended their lead to 10 minutes over their immediate pursuers, whose number had shrunk to eight. The Tour continued amid general jubilation. A wire from L'Auto's correspondent in Saint-Girons reported that, 'There is a copy of L'Auto in every hand, and there is a long ovation whenever our Director Henri Desgrange goes by in his official car.' It was 10:40am. Henri Desgrange resumed his place at the head of the race behind Christophe and the young Buysse, both of whom were showing obvious signs of fatigue. The race was approaching its *dénouement*. The control point in Saint-Girons was about to close when a rumour began to circulate ever more strongly. The wire from Saint-Girons finished on an improbable note: 'Some cyclists who had accompanied the racers on the Col du Portet-d'Aspet are telling us that Lapize has dropped out.'

Lapize had abandoned the race.

Not only had he dropped out, but he had turned round and ridden back the way he had come! Shortly before the summit, a short distance behind Defraye, who had just got himself ahead, he stopped and pointed his handlebars back down the mountain. His only comment, in a flat voice, had been: 'I can't compete in these conditions. All the Belgians are helping Defraye and at the same time helping Alcyon.'

Was it really true? We will never know. But already in the Alps, the young rider Lambot had been accused of giving his compatriot illicit assistance. This Lambot was riding for Le Globe. Furthermore, at the foot of the Portet-d'Aspet, the make-up of the group of eight men could help to explain Lapize's concern. Around him were Defraye, of course, and two other Alcyon riders, Garrigou and Heusghem. The other four, Salmon, Devroye, Mottiat and Coomans, all belonged to Thomann, the Alcyon satellite. So...

So, the outcome was that Defraye won the Luchon stage very nicely, thank you, and the race was decapitated. In a grey and miserable Paris, it was a first triumph in the Tour de France for Belgium, which saw nine of its riders among the first 12 places. And Odile Defraye was in no sense an unworthy addition to the roll of honour.

But we must return to Luchon, because it was Lapize's renunciation that had made the news. The riders themselves said nothing. Christophe, second in the stage (and second in Paris), had only this thought to contribute: 'I have excellent memories of the Thermes at Luchon.' They never saw nothing, m'lud. It is quite another story when it comes to the chroniclers, who refused to let the story drop. In the heat of the moment, the boss Henri Desgrange castigated the French champion: 'The reasons he abandoned the race are, above all, psychological ones.' He placed Lapize in the camp of those stars who are offered a fortune by the big-name brands under the pressure of rampant competition. And he had words of consolation for poor old Hammond, the boss of La Française, who had seen his efforts so poorly rewarded. However, in the heat of the same moment, he was flatly contradicted by Monsieur Hammond himself, who replied in his own way by withdrawing his entire team from the race. He explained his decision in the pages of *L'Écho des Sports*: in other words, in the paper of the opposition. He expressed disappointment, because he had warned Desgrange that Spring about the dangers of recruiting subsidiaries of the big brands. 'We are withdrawing from an unfair contest of one against three, convinced that there is nothing we can do in these conditions. Consider that we have only the one team while Alcyon, as well as its own, has two other sub-brands whose riders, overtly or not, help those of their parent company. This event proves to us that the handicap was too serious to overcome, even for champions like ours. It is a lesson for the future and I promise you that it will not go in vain.'

More pressure…

The incident became a scandal. An offical *commissaire*, Monsieur Benso from Marseille, corroborated the accusations against Alcyon. Desgrange, who was no fool – anything but – bravely admitted that not all was well with his Tour de France. Of the current mess, he said: 'I can assure you that it stems from the conflict between the mind of the man who is in charge of drawing up the rules, and those of the directors of companies that contest the event.' He announced that the 1913 Tour would be different 'for being more tightly controlled.'

It was the beginning of a long, hard struggle. In spite of his determination and relentless efforts, Henri Desgrange did not manage entirely to win his contest against the big brands. It would not be until a full 17 years after the Lapize Affair that he would finally put an end to the conflict with a radical decision. Let me explain.

In 1929, the victory of Dewaele, a Belgian rider for the Alcyon team – fancy meeting them again! – gave rise to general indignation. Completely worn-out a week before the finish, Dewaele, who was brave in the extreme but strangely protected by his direct rivals, and the beneficiary of some 'unusual' assistance, managed to retain his first position all the way to Paris. Desgrange was furious. Alcyon's *directeur sportif* – Ludovic Feuillet, Baugé's heir – had duped him. Monsieur Ludo, as he was known in the business, went too far a few weeks later during the tour of the Basque Country. The French champion, Marcel Bidot of Alcyon, had the race wrapped up two days from the end. But, so as to thumb his nose at Desgrange and to rehabilitate 'his' Tour de France champion, Ludovic Feuillet, who had stayed in Paris, sent his instructions by telegram to Pamplona: 'Order: let Dewaele win.' Dewaele won. Ludo celebrated.

Then Desgrange struck. In 1930, he decreed that teams would no longer be fielded by the cycling brands. From then on, the Tour de France would only invite national teams. Well, I can't help thinking that the spark for this 1930 revolution in Paris was lit in 1912 on the Portet-d'Aspet. At the very moment when the French champion, Octave Lapize, turned back down the mountain.

To return to the current business – July 1912, I mean – the about-turn on the Portet-d'Aspet would mark a significant turning in the French road racing champion's career. He would desert the road altogether, abandoning it for seven months! Out of pique, said those who thought they knew that Lapize had subsequently regretted abandoning the Tour. But all that is pure speculation because, true to form, Octave made no further comment on the matter. As one of his *soigneurs* said shortly afterwards, 'This rider is easy to put up with: he never complains.'

So, he tried a different track: the velodrome circuit. In fact, he was just following fashion: in 1912, even if the Golden Age of track cycling was coming to an end, it was still the dominant force. In Paris, three velodromes opened in the summer: the Buffalo in Neuilly, the Parc des Princes in Boulogne and the Municipal at Vincennes. They took it in turns to organise events, and the sporting public had no fewer than three meetings to entertain them, even without the training sessions which were also highly prized by the public. There were more and more individual matches between sprinters or stayers. The American 'Colored Cyclone' Major Taylor and the Dane Ellegaard were the great sprint attractions. They were pitted against all the local specialists: the Dupré brothers, Friol, Poulain and Hourlier, who had all been or would be French, European or world champions. Motor-paced races offered no less Herculean challenges, notably between Sérès and Darragon. In short, in Paris but also in the regions, you could go from one 'monster programme' to the next, from track to track, and these meetings regularly made the front pages of the specialized newspapers. From the month of August, road racing retired to the inside pages. The road-man Octave Lapize slipped easily into the track racing circuit, where he was hardly an unknown quantity: indeed, he was much in demand, as a kind of special phenomenon: the only rider capable both of vanquishing the Tourmalet and feeling at ease on the concrete or wooden track of the velodrome.

Talking of the Tourmalet, it was at the velodrome in La Louvière in Belgium that he took his revenge on Odile Defraye. On 18 August, just one month after the Portet-d'Aspet, in a four-hour race(!), the French champion crushed the Belgian one, who finished several laps behind. This consolation prize was repeated a little later in Paris, at the French Grand Prix. This was a 100-kilometre race behind tandems, which was easily won by Lapize. He beat Defraye, in fourth place, by 11 laps!

Tandem-paced racing, still called 'racing behind human trainers' at the time, was just made for Lapize. His small size, skill, tactical nouse and turn of speed made him a crack in the discipline. On Thursday 22 August, at the Buffalo, he gave his best ever performance in this specialism. In the course of the same race, he grabbed five world records! *L'Auto* tells the story: 'Lapize had a whale of a time in the 100 kilometres behind tandems: without trainers, in front or behind, we have seen him from every angle now, and always with the same brilliance, the same success.' The race had started fairly slowly, but after a brutal acceleration, the previous best times in the world were beaten one by one: for 60, 70, 80 and 90 kilometres. To round off the display, Octave covered the 100 kilometres in two hours, two minutes, three seconds and four hundredths of a second: a new world record.

He was at it again on 29 September, again at Buffalo, his favourite track. The organisers had set up a match between Lapize and Berthet over an hour behind tandems. It is rare for a world record to be broken during a head-to-head race, but Lapize did it. In that hour, he covered 50.93 kilometres, with Berthet 350 metres behind. The next day's assessment was that 'this was a massive performance; the winner of the Tour de France is a first-rate specialist over genuine middle-distance races, perhaps the best since René Pottier*, to whom he bears a strange likeness.'

So it was that Octave Lapize's new life unfolded over several months, from one velodrome to the next. It was a pleasant life, meticulously organised. It was the ideal way to deal simultaneously with the various pressures on Lapize the racer, the businessman and the man. The better to appreciate this system, I paid a visit myself to the centre of our hero's world: a small triangle in the 10th *arrondissement* of Paris around the Lariboisière Hospital, where everything he needed was to hand. He lived with Juliette, or rather at Juliette's flat (it was registered in her name) at 11 Rue Amboise-Paré, a fine middle-class address. He just had to walk to the end of the street to reach the Gare du Nord, something he did regularly, given all the invitations he received to Belgian velodromes. Finally, he only needed to commute 300 metres each morning to his shop at 112, Boulevard de la Chapelle. Since the business was starting to flourish, the champion kept an eye on his affairs. Lapize cycles, produced by La Française under the Diamant brand, were not only sold in the shops, but also went to equip racing teams that were starting to embark on winning ways, particularly in Belgium.**

It was in Belgium, too, that Octave finished the season. Brussels had effectively outmanoeuvred Paris in the Six Days stakes.

All right, so the Vel' d'Hiv' on the Rue Nelaton had celebrated its reopening on Sunday 27 October. So everyone declared with one voice (at least in Paris) that 'The Palais des Sports, Paris's

---

* René Pottier (1879-1907) had also been an exceptional cyclist. In the 1905 Tour de France he led at the summit of the Ballon d'Alsace, 'to applause from the event's three followers (in a car).' In 1906, he repeated the exploit, this time going one better. He won five stages and the general classification. René Pottier ended his life on 25 January 1907.

** Octave himself never raced on a Lapize cycle. Throughout his entire career, from 1911 onwards, he rode La Française bicycles with the tricolour head badge. In 1923, the Belgian Paul Deman won Paris–Tours on a Lapize cycle.

own Madison Square, is the finest sporting establishment anywhere in the world.' The event was so successful that its management announced two days later that the Paris Six Days would take place from 13 to 19 January 1913. This was the news everybody had been waiting for. For two months, the Six Days would inspire a daily soap opera in the newspapers, reporting who had been signed up, who had withdrawn, the training stories and all the goings-on at the fringes of what they were calling the 'Monster Race'.

None of this altered the fact that the Belgians had got there first. The Brussels Six Days was going ahead at the end of December 1912, albeit by the skin of its teeth. And they had got the signature of Octave Lapize. In Paris, Octave trained assiduously at the Vel' d'Hiv' during the week, taking part in race meetings on Sundays. On 15 December, he faced a head-to-head race against the rising middle-distance star Georges Sérès. To balance their chances, the protagonists were set a contest over three rounds: a speed race over one kilometre which Lapize won by all of 10 centimetres; a 10-kilometre race behind tandems which was also won by Lapize; and a motor-paced race over 10 kilometres that went to Sérès. Lapize, the victor by two wins to one, was given a fine ovation as he made his lap of honour, hand in hand with his opponent.

And then it was time for him to pack his bags for Brussels, where the Six Days were to take place from 20 to 27 December. On a track measuring no more than 125m, the riders prepared for what would be a strange sort of Christmas. The special correspondent from *L'Auto* wrote:

> When he saw the track, which looks like a bowl with a few marbles running round it, Lapize, who is a well-read man, declared: 'It's Hercules' footbath!'.' There were several Frenchmen at the start: Petit-Breton, Charron, Hourlier and Comès, who together made up a team, and Lapize, who was paired with the French sprint champion Victor Dupré, known as 'the giant of Roanne'.

The whole of Brussels was celebrating. Lapize was having great fun and let it be known that his greatest pleasure was chasing behind the pack. Dupré, on the other hand, was having no fun at all. His large build was not made for the hairpin bends. Octave was soon convinced that he would have to renounce any hopes of victory, but willingly turned his hand to helping out his French mates Hourlier and Comès. Suddenly, things ground to a halt. Dupré abandoned, followed by Hourlier. And then Vanhouwaert, the crowd's darling, dropped out as well. Now Lapize was put with Vandenberghe, which was no mean feat in itself. First of all, this Vandenberghe raced for Alcyon's subsidiary Thomann, and had not exactly been neutral in the Defraye Affair on the Tour de France. But that was not all. Vandenberghe had also entered the Six Days, although it had been expressly forbidden by the Alcyon manager, Baugé. Seeing as he was already there, he thought, he might as well go all the way. Lapize was careful not to dampen the enthusiasm of such a zealous team-mate, and so it was that the Lapize-Vandenberghe team won the Brussels Six Days, covering a distance of 4,134.5 kilometres (against 3,851 kilometres in 1911). The second-placed team of Petit-Breton and Comès, also reformed after Hourlier's withdrawal, finished one lap behind.

All the same, you can't but be surprised by the turn of events in that year of 1912. Lapize, who had lost the Tour de France to the Belgians, had now triumphed in the Brussels Six Days – alongside a Belgian. It can be hard to keep up with Octave Lapize, so brilliant on the road as well as the track, from the beginning of February all the way to the end of December.

THREE IN A ROW

From 1912 to 1913, from Brussels to Paris, it was the same story all over again: the same old Six Days hullabaloo. The only new thing about this Six Days was the word 'Paris'.

Superb posters suddenly blossomed everywhere you looked; the newspapers started issuing supplements or even publishing special editions. Reporters flocked to the quayside in Cherbourg to welcome the American specialists as they disembarked from the liner *France*. Day after day, they wrote about the invasion of a tribe of Yanks, led by a chief of giant stature: the Californian Floyd MacFarland, a huge champion turned manager. All the citizens of Paris were informed if the slightest new detail came out during a training session. 'Watched by an army of regulars, the squirrels arrive early at the track and do not leave until very late, even though most of them have already been out on the road in the morning.' Whenever Lapize appeared, wreathed in the glory of his victory in Belgium, it gave rise to all sorts of comments. 'In training, Lapize sports a balaclava in academic colours,' or 'He is mostly training himself to stay in the saddle. He can already go fast, but he is less well-trained where he meets the saddle,' or perhaps, 'Lapize is in good shape, just cooking nicely.' A confident Octave reassured his supporters: 'At the moment, I've had enough sleep to last me a month. It's even getting me down a bit because I feel so heavy I can't do much in training. But don't you worry. As soon as that pistol goes off, I'll be completely transformed and you will see the real Lapize.'

The real Lapize made his appearance on Sunday 5 January, in the Six Hours race. With his team-mate Dupré, he won the event while the favourites, the Australian/American pairing of Goullet and Fogler, were left in fourth place. The fever mounted. After their lap of honour, Dupré and Lapize were lifted up and carried in triumph by the crowd.

To suggest that the Paris Six Days was superior to the Brussels event would be something of an understatement. Five days before the opening, it was declared the finest on the planet. Charles Ravaud said so, in the pages of *L'Auto*:

> Yes, the Paris Six Days has roused the blood of bicycle enthusiasts everywhere. Nobody doubts our reputation now as the home of cycling par excellence.

Charles Ravaud supported his argument with technical reasons: 'A perfect track measuring 250 metres and a firm, sensible set of rules.'

I have to tell you something. In those exceptional days, Ravaud the journalist became Monsieur Ravaud, named as the *directeur de piste* or referee. He was quite right to stress the minute precision of the regulations' 26 articles, which were less flexible than the ones in Madison Square in New York. It became obligatory for riders on the same team to wear identical jerseys. On top, the first rider had to wear a blue number on a white background, and the second a white number on a blue background. The rules stipulated that the race would take place over six whole days, or 144 hours consecutively. The start would be given on Monday 13 January at 6pm, after which the teams of two riders would relay each other when they liked, American-style.

On 13 January at 6 o'clock in the evening, 15 teams lined up at the start, in the warm atmosphere of the Vel d'Hiv: two teams were American, two Belgian, one Italian, eight French and two mixed. Of the latter, it was the Goullet-Fogler team that was most hotly tipped, in spite of their disappointment in the Six Hours. Lapize knew all about Fogler. He was the American who had won in New York in 1911, the year the young French champion had discovered America. Goullet, meanwhile, was considered a phenomenon. At 21 years old, many people were calling him the best sprinter in the world.

How best to describe the event? First, let us talk about the money. There was money everywhere: ticket sales were booming; the bonuses on offer were magnificent. As a popular success, it was beyond all expectations. But we should mention the race itself, all the same. The public enjoyed the spectacle and gave its hearty applause, but did not really understand the subtleties of an event that it was seeing for the first time. The Europeans gave it their all, but the MacFarland Boys were uncompromising: they stuck together and did not let a single team go a lap ahead. And the spectators were surprised, if not disappointed, to see after 143 hours that the first six teams were still on the same lap. As chance would have it, there were four French teams still going strong at this point: Brocco-Berthet, Petit-Breton-Georget, Cruppelandt-Godivier and above all Dupré-Lapize.

This was the moment when the referee Ravaud appealed to article 24, paragraph 2: 'At the last pistol shot announcing the 144th hour, all riders, without exception, will leave the track. If several teams are in the lead with an equal number of laps, their designated representatives for the sprint will line up for a race of 10 laps (2,500 metres) to determine the outcome of the race.

It was the sprinters, of course, who were kept back for this finale and the crowd wanted to believe that Dupré had a good chance. Lapize had ridden by himself for long periods to give his team-mate a chance to conserve energy. But it was in vain: Goullet was too strong, and beat Dupré by a length to win the first Paris Six Days. The final classification read as follows:

1st Goullet-Fogler
2nd Dupré-Lapize
3rd Walthour-Wiley, an American pair

It had been a fast and regular race. By covering 4,467.58 kilometres in the 144 hours, the winners had established a record that would never be broken. What's more, with his French ancestry, the young Australian Goullet had all the right credentials.

Octave could have expressed disappointment at losing, when he had come so close – within a single length, after almost 4,500 kilometres – to such a historic victory. Not at all, he said, declaring himself well satisfied. He returned to the Vel d'Hiv on 4 March for the Racing Cyclists' Friendly Insurance Society competition. With Friol, he was the Vice-President of this Society, and was quite proud of its new constitution, which guaranteed emergency assistance – such as doctors' visits and medical bills – for an annual subscription of 24 francs. On this note, he took his leave of the velodromes for the season and headed for the open road.

Road racing had not left the news: quite the reverse, in fact. The Belgians, having stretched their wings, were keen to take on their big neighbours. A certain Karel Van Wijnandaele came up with a race called the Ronde Van Vlaanderen. Very soon, the inventor and his race would become an indispensable part of the racing calendar under the name of the Tour of Flanders. In France, transfers were all the rage. First at Alcyon with Baugé, then at Automoto without him, Faber moved with Baugé to Peugeot. His training régime was as outrageous as ever. In February, to put the finishing touches to their preparations, Faber and a few of his team-mates, including the Italian Micheletto, rode in short stages from Nice to Paris – via Bordeaux. For Baugé, the main thing was not to miss their grand entrance on 23 March, the day of Paris–Roubaix. On the track in Roubaix, Faber won the sprint ahead of the six riders in his wake. With his incredible 78 inch gear (26 x 9), compared with a maximum of 69 inch among his rivals, big François had not given anyone else the trouble of setting the pace. Consequently, (a) the average speed of the race was 35.53 kph, which would not be surpassed until 1931, and (b) unlucky riders were irrevocably left behind.

Lapize was one of those who fell victim to punctures. He won a commendation for sportsmanship in the press the following morning: 'This did not prevent him, let us point out *en passant*, from behaving as befits a great rider, refusing to abandon the race until the game was up.'

Paris–Tours, on 6 April, was billed as the revenge match for Paris–Roubaix. This turned out to be truer than anyone thought. This time, Faber punctured – at which, of course, the La Française team took off. A 40-strong peloton swept through Blois, then Amboise, before arriving *en masse* at the velodrome in Tours. There, it was panic stations because the river Cher had burst its banks and flooded the public enclosure. The water had spread on to the track just where the riders who had made their first lap were being joined by others arriving at the velodrome. In the ensuing chaos, the race officials decided to judge the winners as far as they could and then call a tie for the remaining riders. On the second of the three laps, Lapize, in a good position, was just putting on a burst of speed when a great cry went up. Obstructed by the Belgian Messelis, the French champion fell, and the race was won by his team-mate Cruppelandt.

Disappointed, Octave decided to enter Paris-Menen on 20 April, a race in its fourth edition which he had hitherto overlooked. Organised by the Menen Velodrome, this race was what we would call a semi-classic. It ran more or less along the Paris–Roubaix route, extended by some 20 kilometres, since Menen was just the other side of the border. The contestants ran into a violent headwind from the very outset. In Amiens, there were only 26 at the front, whittled down to five in Arras, and just two in Béthune: Lapize and the Belgian Monseur, who were riding at over 30 kph.

Seven hundred metres before the final control point in La Chapelle-d'Armentières, the two men decided to stop 'to answer a call of nature.' Monseur got straight back in the saddle, but not Lapize. He abandoned the race. We will never know the reasons for this mysterious withdrawal. For the record, Monseur was caught by the lone rider Micheletto, who would beat him in the sprint.

Milan–San Remo was no more destined to help lift Octave's morale. The Italians placed him among the favourites but, alas, he had another fall and had to pull out. The failure was all the harder to take since the race was won by his earlier 'enemy', Odile Defraye, winner of the 1912 Tour. Bordeaux–Paris, on 17 May, the race nobody thought could suit *le Frisé** would only add to his distress. Once again, the third time in a row, Octave dropped out before Orléans.

This was the first year that the name of Lapize had not been linked with victory in one of the big races by the end of May. The first of June came round just at the right moment.

In the French 100-kilometre championships, the reigning French champion rediscovered the sweet scent of victory. Reaching the top of the ascent at Minières with a lead of three minutes over his La Française team-mates Brocco and Cruppelandt, Lapize established a new record in the event, at two hours, 40 minutes and 50 seconds, representing an average speed of 37.2 kph. He enjoyed his three laps of honour of the Parc des Princes, wearing the tricolour jersey for the third time. To go with his Paris–Roubaix hat trick of 1909-1910-1911, he had done the triple in the national championships of 1910, 1911 and 1912. He forgot all about both his disappointing start to the season and the desire to 'call it a day' that he was supposed to have confided to his close friends. He was pumped-up and raring to go as he prepared for Paris–Brussels, on the calendar for the following Sunday, 8 June. A fall in training – more shock than damage – did nothing to put the brakes on his enthusiasm. He had a soft spot for this race because he was its 'local lad': for seven years now, Paris–Brussels had started in Villiers-sur-Marne. Octave, the boy from Villiers, could show his colleagues round as they made their preparations on the Saturday for a

---

* Lapize's nickname, meaning 'Curly'

1 a.m. start. The Peugeot team set up camp at the Café Barré, Alcyon at the Café Meignan, and La Française, of course, at the Café Séminel. All of these cyclists' rendez-vous were located along Villiers' main street, the Rue de Paris. Discreet as ever, Octave would have omitted to mention that the fine house at number 61 had recently come into his ownership.

Nor did he give away his intention to attack from the off, in a race whose length called for a prudent approach: there was a little matter of 440 kilometres to cover. In Épernay (130 kilometres) the pack still consisted of 55 riders, but this had been reduced to 28 by the time they reached the 200-kilometre mark in Bethel. In Namur (350 kilometres) there were 20 and, at Wavre, only eight left! In Brussels, the finishing line was on an airfield: an odd kind of finish for the riders arriving along a grass track, 1,800m long, protected by mounted gendarmes who were having some trouble holding back the crowds of excited spectators. In torrential rain, five riders came through for a sprint finish, which was won by Lapize from his La Française comrades Vanhouwaert and Cruppelandt. It was a triumph – the only way to describe it – for Lapize, because this win was his third hat trick, after Paris–Roubaix and the French championship. He was now the victor of three consecutive Paris–Brussels (1911, 1912, 1913).

The June's events had weakened his earlier resolution to attend increasingly to his cycle business. And seeing as the Tour de France was around the corner, it was a case of *'Vive le Tour!'*

As promised, Henri Desgrange had made some significant modifications to his event. For the first time, the route would run from West to East, crossing the Pyrenees before the Alps. But the biggest change was that the classification would be by cumulative time and not on points. It is nonetheless rather curious that Desgrange the innovator also felt it necessary to take the retrograde step of imposing fixed gears for the 470-kilometre Brest-La Rochelle stage.

At the moment of its launch on 29 June, this Tour de France celebrated a double record for participation, with 140 riders taking part, 51 of them as *groupés* in nine teams, and a much greater number of race followers. For the first time, observers started to speak of them as the 'caravan'.

The Italian Micheletto won the first stage in Le Havre, and the Belgian Messelis took the second, in Cherbourg. It went to a sprint each time, where Lapize was conspicuous by his absence. Everyone was waiting for something special on the third Cherbourg-Brest stage, which was both long and hilly. They would not be disappointed.

At the control point in Guingamp, there was no sign of Lapize. Lapize had disappeared. The reporters from the *Dépêche de Brest* and the Rennes *Ouest-Éclair* had seen nothing, and neither had the majority of the race followers, who were to condemn the French champion the following day. They had *L'Écho des Sports* to thank for the scoop on Lapize's desertion. After Saint-Brieuc, the peloton struggled up the long climb at Trémuson, and the newspaper's 'all-seeing, all-knowing and all-saying' correspondent was having a wonderful time.

> No sooner had they reached the edge of the village, having dropped Faber and Christophe, the whole pack set off at a sprint, apart from Lapize, whose front tyre had just punctured. The tricolour jersey stopped, dejected, on the central reservation. He mended the puncture, but seemed in no hurry, because three minutes went by before he set off again. For a quarter of an hour, he attempted to close the gap separating him from the leaders, but it was a waste of time. Realizing this, Lapize buried himself in an auberge, firmly set on abandoning the race. Unfortunately, he had not thought to bring his bicycle in with him. A bike with a tricolour head badge leaning against the door of a bistro was enough to attract the attention of the great lion tamer himself [read 'Desgrange']! Out he came from the central cage to give a sermon to the

man called 'Tatave', who came outside with him a few minutes later. Lapize remounted, but as soon as the hearse [read 'Desgrange's car'] was out of view, he did the same thing again, this time next to a building that was not quite so exposed as the last one. And the victor of Paris–Brussels, whose intentions, by the way, we had called into question well in advance of the Tour, sat down in front of a nice bowl of onion soup!

L'Écho des Sports no doubt allowed itself a little artistic licence.

In Brest, where the stage was won by Pélissier, the scandal over Lapize's withdrawal took on another dimension. The La Française team and its subsidiary Liberator withdrew from the race. The Director, Monsieur Hammond, was not present on the Tour de France that year, so it was with a certain distance, but also in a firm tone that he issued his verdict: 'I was only half-surprised when Lapize abandoned the Tour,' he said. 'This rider had the stomach neither for Bordeaux–Paris nor the Tour de France. He only came, against our wishes, because of a strange contradiction: while he repeatedly said that he was taking part without conviction, he really did want to race. And since his contract allowed this, we had to honour it. Now, to say that I was satisfied with this way of proceeding would obviously be an exaggeration.'

The press in general and Henri Desgrange in particular were very harsh in their opinions, pointing out that Lapize's selfish behaviour had eliminated his team-mate Émile Georget from a race he could still have hoped to win.* In short, everyone agreed that the French champion had finally lost his pedals. It was not the case.

---

* The Tour de France was won by the 23 year-old Belgian Philippe Thys, completing the success of a formidable Peugeot team, all of whose members finished the race. Only 25 riders made it as far as the Parc des Princes.

But it is true to say that Lapize was beginning to let his pedals slip. The racer was gradually giving way to the businessman. Listening to Monsieur Hammond, it is clear that the contract binding Octave to La Française was more than just a racing contract. La Française was using the Lapize brand name to manufacture cycles, but also shoes and other cycling accessories listed 25th and 26th in the national register of patent rights, including 'bicycle toeclips and quick-release clasps for toe-straps'.*

In a word, the man Lapize, while still appearing on the road and on the track, was already elsewhere. He had realized that, if he wanted to be elsewhere, it was more convenient to stick to the track. So, he did not take part in the Tour of Lombardy at the end of the season. His colleagues in this new world were not *routiers* called Garrigou, Christophe or Faber, but the *pistards* (track riders) Hourlier, Comès and Berthet. But there was no sense in

---

* Octave was personally involved in the running of his shop, holding the position of Director responsible for manufacture, promotion and sales. In his 1912 catalogue – whose cover bore a colour picture of the champion in his tricolour jersey – this is how he announced the production of a blue model with red head tube.

Dear Clients,
I have the honour to present to you the most recent bicycles I have built and which I am launching onto the market under the name Octave Lapize Cycles.
Permit me to draw your attention to the special models I have constructed, using all the experience I have acquired through riding to victory on the highest-quality cycles… I have therefore created two models which I hope will meet with your hearty approval.
    a road-racing bicycle
    a light touring racer
These two machines are assembled using one-piece welded frames and extra-rigid reinforced tubes… I have certified for myself that while they are lighter, these frames are superior to those with brazed joints, when it comes to assembly and solidity…
With all their advantages, my machines are sold at prices that defy any competition of comparable quality. When you consult this catalogue, you will also come to realize the modest prices of my tyres and accessories.
    In the hope that you will wish to honour me with your orders I remain, valued Clients, your dedicated
    O. Lapize

which he had come down in the world. This was the moment that Berthet took the world hour record to 43.78 kilometres, at the Buffalo track. To appreciate this performance in full, you must consider that the great Fausto Coppi would only cover two kilometres more, on a fast wooden track in 1942.

For the winter season at the Vel' d'Hiv', Lapize found himself a new team-mate for the American races and the Six Days: the Italian Oliveri became his partner. They had already triumphed together in regional events, notably in Tours, in a velodrome that had been full to bursting. Even more convincingly, the Oliveri-Lapize pairing were runners-up in the 24-hour American-style race at Paris's Vel' d'Hiv', behind Hourlier-Comès. What a race that was! Seven teams arrived together on the same lap at the finish, having covered 873.5 kilometres. Finally, Lapize notched up individual successes (albeit minor ones, I admit), mostly behind a tandem.

However, with the benefit of hindsight, we can see that his most significant performance was on Sunday 18 October, in the season's closing event at the Buffalo Velodrome. On that day, Lapize took up and won a remarkable head-to-head match, where he had everything to lose, against Franck Henri. This Franck Henri deserves an explanation.

The match pitted the year's two French champions against one another: the professional and the independent, the master and the pupil, both equally gifted. Lapize needs no introduction, of course, but the moment has come to introduce Henri, the forgotten man of cycling history. He was a 21 year-old from the Levallois Vélo-Club, and therefore under the tutelage of the already-famous Paul Ruinart. In 1913, in his category, he had not only won the French championship, but also Paris–Roubaix, Paris–Tours, Paris-Évreux, the Circuit du Midi and a few other trifles. In his 1937 *Memoirs*, Paul Ruinart sketched a portrait of his prodigy in these words:

> He was a tough Breton from Landerneau, where he had worked as a mechanic. His father, a gardener by

trade, was of pure Armorican stock, but his mother was English. His real name was François, but his mother called him Franck and the name stuck. Physically, he was thickset, broad in the chest and shoulders, with massive thighs and a forceful face under a stubborn forehead. A superb racer on the flat, an excellent climber and a fearsome sprinter, he was terribly pig-headed and even pretty gruff. He did not trust a soul, even his team-mates. In the tribe of the amateurs, Franck Henri really laid down the law.

Looking at his photograph, I will only add that Franck Henri also sported a great mop of hair and in many ways resembled the young Octave. Moreover, like Petit-Breton, Faber and many others, Lapize predicted great things in the young Breton's future professional career. Alas, as Paul Ruinart relates, with a wealth of horrific detail, 'Franck Henri was killed in the first months of the war by a grenade which exploded prematurely.'

The match on 18 October 1913 nicely illustrates a preoccupation of the time. The French Cycling Union was asking itself questions about the future, the health and the image of cycling. Indeed, it sent a questionnaire to a number of favoured representatives, of which Henri Desgrange was one. As a journalist, he naturally responded in the pages of *L'Auto*, writing 'What the racing cyclist should be like':

> The legend has been born, gained ground and continues to circulate, that cycling is only for scallywags. This is a bit much, if you consider that very soon two million bicycles will be paying tax.*
>
> I would like the cyclist to be a charming person, as far from being a snob as from a greedy brute eating up the miles and wiping his nose on his hand. I would

---

* Anyone buying a bicycle had to pay a stamp: basically, a tax disc.

like him to be liberated by the bicycle from all life's platitudes and pettiness...

I don't want to see heads with perfect partings, but neither do I want dishevelled mops. No cocktail parties, and no 'bevvies' at lunchtime: not prudes, but not womanisers either. I want him to be a man of action without doubts, a modern man, able to walk into the future hand in hand with a partner as liberated as he is.'

Henri Desgrange seems to have had a semi-angelic, semi-aristocratic vision of the cyclist. But strangely enough, his imaginary portrait reminds me of somebody I know. A real man.

Second portrait

It was the end of 1913.

Since 6pm on 24 October, Octave was 26 years old. Only 26, with all his future ahead of him.

Everything moved quickly with Lapize. Since he had burst onto the track at Roubaix in 1909, it had only taken him four years to establish his supremacy on the road and, at the same time, his presence on the track. At 26, he was a champion at the peak of his powers. He was also a champion apart, in that he enjoyed more notoriety than popularity. Yes, there were times when he was called 'le Frisé' by the papers or his rivals, or 'Tatave' by the inner circle of his family and the top echelons of the Vel' d'Hiv', but he did nothing to make himself more popular. And he was not really popular: he was too much top of the class, too clever, too lucky, too strong to be idolized.

Above all, he was too sober. He never showed off, or even really put on a show. Apart from the 'Murderers' episode on the Aubisque, he never raised his voice and never moaned. If he ever allowed himself a touch of malice, it was in private. Thus, at the finish of the 1911 Paris–Brussels, he put his own questions to the interviewer and answered as it suited him. With just the hint of a tease, he thanked the speechless journalist for having given him an interview.

Lapize's greatest asset as a racer was his intelligence. He instinctively adapted to the innovations in cycling equipment.

He devloped the cycling shoes, toe-clips and straps that were sold in his name. Lapize was a brand. Like another refined cyclist, Émile Georget, he was shrewd enough to exploit the benefits of the freewheel, able to optimize his pedalling better than others and to conserve muscle power, managing his rest times during races, and thus refining his tactics. Lapize the racer was too astute to stick with the 'slave wheel'. The freewheel was his thing, and dare I suggest that Lapize was a kind of Asterix, outwitting 'Gearfix'.

Octave had given a good deal of thought to his profession. He had signed, and therefore approved (if not written himself) a long text on the subject of road cycling printed in a special edition of *La Vie au Grand Air*. This article set out his thinking about diet and training. With his rather brutal frankness, he weighs straight in: 'There is no such thing as a special diet for the road racer.' Strike one! Further on, he declares that training has to be an 'obligatory, extremely strict, exacting preparation'. Strike two! Next comes the critical analysis. 'A diet involves following the principle of rigorously worked-out food intake and great regularity in the taking of meals. However, in reality you are woken each day in time for the start of races at different times, meaning that mealtimes are constantly changing – not to mention the climatic variations which are at work from one day to the next on individuals experiencing great nervous tension, and pyschologically susceptible to sudden changes in the weather.' Neither does Octave Lapize advocate a strict diet in the run-up to a race. He is mistrustful of 'acquired habits governing every aspect of life (sleep, food, rest) because, to be blunt, circumstances will force you to abandon them. And then a new sort of life begins, regulated differently or rather, not regulated at all. No diets, then, during races because it is not possible; no diets beforehand in order to avoid having to suddenly change your habits.'

The Lapize Method is quite simple: keep to your own diet, every day (his weight only ever varied by two kilogrammes at the very most). 'The best way is to listen to Nature. You just have to give the stomach what it asks for, what it can easily digest, and each individual need only be guided by his own constitution.' (A good deal was already known in 1913. For example, in its weekly medical column, *Sporting* magazine published an article explaining the rôle of carbohydrates in muscle activity.) Lapize also recommended that, 'Food, during an event, should be in substantial quantities, and even a little spicy, to meet the demands of repetitive and prolonged effort. An individual in these circumstances will not be sustained by a mild diet. He needs a little 'crack of the whip'. To me, as well as to many others, the system sometimes recommended of drinking milk and Vichy mineral water has nothing at all to recommend it. Adopting this method is a sure route to depression. Coffee is an excellent stimulant, and a drop of alcohol does no harm. Alcohol! In reality, almost everyone takes it, but nobody admits to it.' Let's not split hairs: the word 'doping' would be invented in 1921.

And what about training? Lapize takes a formal approach: 'Whatever one's natural physical abilities, it is impossible to keep going from start to finish unless you have reached peak fitness through a sustained programme of training. It follows that you have to be on the road every day and cover a minimum of 100 kilometres. Apart from extreme meteorological events, the road racer has to get used to cycling *in all weathers*. This is how to aquire the powers of endurance he needs to brave the – sometimes unbridled – elements. You should train on all types of terrain, and even pick out the most difficult routes, where a man has to work hardest and longest. And you need to cover such routes at a smart pace. Subjecting yourself to difficulties is an excellent schooling in energy.' By including speed sessions on the track in his training programme, Lapize – who was in any case too fragile in the seat to pedal for hours and hours – prioritized quality over quantity.

The Lapize system was to be a racer *every day*, from one end of the year to the other. This permanent racer's lifestyle suited him all the more since he was equally at home on the track and the road (the names Van Steenbergen and Merckx also come to mind). What made Lapize special was his versatility. We can only salute the success of the multidisciplinary system that allowed him to win Paris–Roubaix and the Tour de France, but also the Brussels Six Days and the world hour record behind a tandem (50.93 kilometres).

His versatility and his success allowed Lapize more turns than most to collect his money past Go. He was suspected of earning a packet, and it was true: he did. In December 1912, *L'Écho des Sports* published – for the first time ever – a balance sheet for the season at the Buffalo velodrome, rigorously calculating what the riders were paid, including prizes and bonuses. The list of the top 50 beneficiaries includes the names of just two road racers: Octave Lapize and Émile Georget. Octave appears at number seven behind six track specialists: four stayers, who were in greatest demand, and the sprinters Ellegaard and Dupré. At the Buffalo velodrome alone, Lapize won 2,405 francs. 'Just for turning up,' you could say.

Henri Desgrange, who granted only 5,000 francs to the winner of the Tour de France, was convinced that easy money from the velodromes was distorting the champions' sporting natures. He claimed that Lapize was obsessed by money and thought about nothing else. One could reply that the young Octave had had it drummed into him by his father that he needed 'first, a stable income!', and that he had developed the habit of counting his pennies early on. And investing them prudently for the years to come. One could point out that Lapize was not, in fact, obsessed with 'his' money. Far from being ungrateful, he had an important rôle as Vice-President of the Racing Cyclists' Friendly Society (by its Constitution, the President had to be a figure from outside the peloton). This organisation was not on the scale of a real trade union, but did come to the assistance of the most needy. It should be said that such social initiatives were beneath the attention of Henri Desgrange. All the same, at 26 years of age, Lapize was showing himself to be a responsible man.

Lapize the racer had changed greatly since his début, and so had the man. He cut an elegant figure, dressed by Sieg on the Avenue de la Grande-Armée (this was advertising). He made use of his moustache, which he shaved or cultivated depending on the occasion. In the tricolour jersey – his work uniform for three years – and under the watchful eye of Juliette, who moved in dressmaking circles and was always nicely turned-out, he always looked good on the road or in town. Charles Ravaud called him 'a gentleman who is able to appear in society, where he is not at all out of place.'

> He is the intellectual of the peloton: he has the head and the legs, that double attribute that you so rarely encounter in cycling champions. He belongs to the company of riders who have helped raise the profile of the professional champion.

Sober in the exercise of his profession, Octave Lapize was discreet when it came to his personal life. A handsome man, he appealed to the ladies, and received letters from his admirers at his private address: 'Vélodrome d'Hiver, rue Nélaton'. Such as the woman, of distinguished appearance, posing next to him in a car at the finish of a race.

But more importantly, or at least more surprisingly, there was one woman who occupied a most dramatic, if not a central place in the lives of the Lapize family, Octave included. Yvonne confirmed this to me: 'Ah! My godmother, Aunt Alice! She was so beautiful, and so kind to me.' Aunt Alice was not exactly Yvonne's aunt, but she really was Octave's cousin (to return to Chapter One: Alice was the daughter of Mathilde Lapize, who had run away from Mende and from the convent, following her brother Jules Octave to Paris).

Now, this Aunt Alice was also known – best known, in fact – as Alicia Delyzia, a star of the music hall. A captain of chorus girls, she had a great reputation in London, where she was appearing at that time in the new revue *More!* at the Ambassador Theatre. Very appropriate, whispered Yvonne to me: Aunt Alice had had plenty of husbands, but the last one was a real Ambassador. It was even said – although without any real evidence – that this marriage had made her a Lady.

In any case, Octave had great admiration and a very soft spot for cousin Alice. Whenever she came to Paris, Alice would drop into the shop on the Boulevard de la Chapelle to hear the latest news of her cousin. In 1917, she sent him a signed photograph: a magnificent portrait, with an inscription in the handwriting of a star: 'For you, my dear little Tatave. Good luck.'

What a family! It must have been quite something for the Lapizes to have two such big stars in their midst, and you can imagine what today's paparazzi would have made of it.

It was the end of 1913.

Since 6pm on 24 October, Octave was 26. *Already* 26. Suffice it to say that he was planning for the future, and there were several indications to suggest that this future might not necessarily involve cycling.

1914, AND THEN...

At the beginning of 1914, the Vel' d'Hiv on Rue Nélaton was once again the epicentre of the cycling world. The festivities, at the start of a New Year that some thought would not bring much joy, had hardly finished when Paris was getting ready for its second Six Days. The winning formula was unchanged. The MacFarland Boys, then, were back, but they did not hesitate to change a winning team. They dissolved the victorious team of 1913. Now, Goullet was racing with a fellow Australian named Grenda, and Fogler with another distinguished American rider, Moran. There were no fewer than ten French teams, in which we might include the Lapize-Oliveri team, since the latter was more of a Marseillais than an Italian. There were also four Belgian teams (the last Tour de France winner, Philippe Thys, would abandon the race before the end) and one from Germany.

All in all, on 12 January 1914, there was a sizeable pack of 20 teams at the start. It was an interesting race and impeccably run, but there were just a few signs of the trouble to come in this kind of race. The public wanted a good show, and everyone was called upon to play his part. Lapize – or 'Tatave' to the top gallery of the velodrome – was sure to sound the alarm whenever a rider attempted an unexpected breakaway during the hours of calm. But he was outclassed in this area by Comès, team-mate and brother-in-law of the speed ace Hourlier. Comès was in cahoots with the police brass band leading the festivities on the central pitch. Whenever he was about to attack, he would raise his arm and the band would launch into a frenzied rendition of the military march *Sambre et Meuse*. The public wanted more.

And then there were the agreements, the understandings, the suspicions. When Brocco found himself on his own after his team-mate Dupré had pulled out, it was suggested that he carry on with a new partner, the excellent Australian rider Clark. But he was so afraid of the Europeans' reaction, who would suspect him of conniving with the Americans, that he opted to withdraw.

Still, as in the previous year, it was a close-run thing and the race went once again to a final sprint, since ten teams had finished on the same lap after 143 hours. This time, though, Goullet met his match. In a masterly performance, Hourlier won the final hour's deciding sprint. The French Hourlier-Comès team took the Six Days after covering 240 kilometres less than in 1913, but this was an insignificant detail. The Oliveri-Lapize team came in seventh. Giuseppe Oliveri, who was more of a bonus chaser than a true sprinter, repeated *ad infinitum* that Lapize was the best man on the track. He was at least the best of the five or six road racers taking part in this meeting of *pistards*.

The striking thing is that opinions of the Six Days began to diverge at only its second edition. Henri Desgrange's *L'Auto* could not but take a rosy view of events at his Vel' d'Hiv'. In *L'Écho des Sports*, Victor Breyer admitted that, 'It's as fine in Paris as it is at Madison Square,' but added that, 'You will see that this exhibition of snobbishness will not last very long. I see nothing about it to suggest longevity.' Six Day races did last, however.

Sporting magazine was the most critical.

> Popular success has come to be the measure of heightened interest in the event. But do these dense crowds, flocking to the ticket counters at the Rue Nélaton, really represent the sporting public, in a strict sense? I have no hesitation in replying that they do not. Whether in the enclosure at twelve francs a ticket or up in the gods for two francs, the

majority of these spectators came out of curiosity, lured by the marvellous publicity surrounding this event. Six days, six days. Throughout this time, it has been sheer madness. From the barber to the café waiter, the question on all their lips was, 'What's the latest?' Well, it takes some nerve to say it, but sport prescribed in such doses is no longer really sport. It's simply spectacle, and risks bringing sport itself into serious danger. At the moment, certain phases of the race are described under the general heading of 'tactical requirements'. There are grounds for fearing that, through abuse, these subtleties could some day degenerate into a vulgar sham.

There is a lot of truth in this, but the madness continued all the same. Seeing the success in Paris – where people had been turned away on some evenings – the Brussels organisers were determined to improve on the previous year. The public had been fired up by the Belgian star Cyril Vanhouwaert, who had wavered for a long time before finally signing up, and by Lapize, who had won the prologue, an individual race over 40 kilometres.

On 2 February 16 teams, including two American ones, set off on a six-day jaunt that would delight the public. Octave had teamed up with fellow countryman Jule Miquel, a middle-distance specialist. The remarkable thing about Miquel was that his greatest successes had been in Germany. In 1913, he had won the Grand Prix in Cologne and Leipzig, hailed as glorious victories against the backdrop of growing Franco-German tension. Just before being paired with Lapize, he had finished second in the Berlin Six Days with the Dutchman Stol. This Stol was so highly rated by his peers that Vanhouwaert had insisted on having him at his side for the Brussels Six Days. It was take it or leave it.

The race was rough, fast and lively. It came alight on the third day when three teams – Lapize-Miguel, MacNamara-Moran and Root-Thomas – managed to get a lap ahead. But the race referee refused to validate the advantage and, as so often, the result came down to a final sprint over 40 laps or five kilometres, to decide between the seven leading teams. Lapize was selected for the final assault. He finished second by a wheel to the formidable Stol, who justified Vanhouwaert's choice of partner. Belgium was in raptures. Beyond the jingoistic rejoicing, it must be noted that the winners had beaten the distance record by covering 4,502.2 kilometres in the 144 hours.

And Lapize? He went on to give a different sort of performance. There had been some doubt as to whether he would make it, just two days after this demanding race, to the annual fête of the Racers' Friendly Society in Paris. It was ill founded. Octave did turn up in spite of the fatigue, unlike many other champions who did not deem it worthwhile to put themselves out.

Beyond the velodromes, such petty squabbles paled into insignificance. In February 1914, the French had more serious concerns. The imminent parliamentary elections provoked political debates that were dominated by international affairs. The German and Russian Empires appeared as so many threats at the gates of France. Three-year military service was brought in, because 'the German barracks are much fuller than the French.' Siren voices were heard to say that war was inevitable, while others protested that it should be avoided at all cost.

There is no evidence to suggest that Lapize was more worried about the situation than anyone else. But we might as well accept straight away that the road racing season would prove a disappointing one for Lapize. Why? Well, it could be suggested that riding two six-day races in quick succession, late in the winter, is hardly the best preparation. At the time, this was not accepted wisdom, because the six days were such a new phenomenon. Moreover, things were not quite so simple, because the principle did not hold true for everyone.

Charles Cruppelandt, for instance. Lapize's team-mate at La Française since 1911 had also taken part in both the Paris and Brussels Six Days, coming in an honourable fourth place each time. He would go on that Spring to become the leading Frenchman on the road, winning Paris–Roubaix and the French championship, and coming third in Milan–San Remo: three events where Lapize hardly featured. On 12 April, he was wearing number one in Suresnes, the starting point for Paris–Roubaix. He appeared in the lead at Beauvais, and again at Doullens, where for the first time the climb did not prove decisive. In Arras, he was seen in the still-intact pack of 40 riders. He abandoned the race at Hénin-Liétard, 45 kilometres from Roubaix. On 10 May, the French Championship brought Lapize a huge disappointment. He did finish the race, in fourth place, but he lost the tricolour jersey he had worn since June 1911. Small consolation that his record in this race, contested over the same 100-kilometre route – two hours, 40 minutes and 56 seconds – remained unbroken.

On 7 June, in foul weather, Octave was back in Villiers-sur-Marne for the start of Paris–Brussels. This was another trophy he was defending, his last chance to extend an unbeaten run. He competed bravely, digging in hard in the driving rain, and reached Namur in a good position. But he was dropped on the climb to the Citadel – and pulled out of the race. For the first time, there was a Belgian winner in Paris–Brussels. And again for the first time, a Swiss, Oscar Egg, had won Paris–Tours. This same Oscar Egg, at only 23, won universal acclaim by taking the world hour record above 44 kilometres. On 18 June, at the Buffalo track, he covered 44.25 kilometres in the 60 minutes, obliterating the performance by Berthet. All this just ten days before the Tour de France.

The 1914 Tour was much like the previous year's, both in its regulation (classification by time) and its route. One change was made in favour of Marseilles, which won back the ville-étape status it had been forced to cede to Aix in 1913. The level of participation, on the other hand, was quite unprecedented. All the cracks were there, from the previous year's victor, Thys, to the former winners Trousselier (1905), Petit-Breton (1907 and 1908), Faber (1909), Lapize (1910), Garrigou (1911) and

Defraye (1912). The Automoto team had recruited a young Italian of 21 who was already national champion. Nobody knew yet that he would turn out to be the first *Campionissimo* in cycling history. His name was Girardengo.

On 28 June 1914, at three o'clock in the morning, at the foot of the slope in Saint-Cloud, Octave Lapize and 142 other riders started the 12th Tour de France. In fact, there were several Lapizes at the *Grand Départ*: the racer Octave, of course, but also O. Lapize the businessman. Advertisements announced that 'Lapize toe-clips and straps are used by every rider on the Tour,' or 'The Lapize air pump – 10 francs apiece – is the technical development of the year.' There was also Octave the worried son, preoccupied by his mother's ill health. And last, but not least, Octave Lapize, the oh-so-attentive companion of Juliette, who was 'expecting a happy event.'

On the afternoon of 28 June 1914, Philippe Thys took the first stage in Le Havre. But it was not Le Havre making the news that day. It was events in Sarajevo, Bosnia-Herzegovina. On that very day, Archduke Franz Ferdinand, heir to the Austro-Hungarian Hapsburg throne, was assassinated by a Bosnian patriot from Serbia. The stormcloud that had been drifting over Europe had suddenly burst. Just a few hours earlier, and the Tour de France might never have taken place. But the Tour was underway.

And it carried on. With no great surprises, but in scorching heat, which was hard for the race followers to bear. In Bayonne, Thys was joint first in the general classification with his compatriot Rossius. Henri Pélissier was third at five minutes, and Lapize fourth at 17 minutes. On the eve of the big Pyrenean mountain stage, he was 'glowing with health and resolved to do the impossible to take the lead in the classification.' Between Bayonne and Luchon, he made a good ascent of the col d'Aubisque, but faded on the Tourmalet. He had to give up all hope of ultimate victory, but he carried on anyway. Without much enthusiasm, perhaps, but with surprising stubbornness, given his aversion towards lost causes. The eighth stage – 370 kilometres from Perpignan to Marseilles – was ridden in tropical heat. Unsurprisingly, the stage was becoming fairly sluggish by the time 25 riders arrived together for the finish in a jam-packed velodrome (people had been turned away and an army of *gendarmes* was stationed on the Prado). The race officials decided that the victor would be decided by a knockout speed contest between these 25 valiant riders: four qualifiers, two semifinals of four riders each, and another four-man final. Lapize went through, together with Brocco, Egg and Engel. The deciding match was a turbulent one, where it was clear that Lapize came in for some rough treatment from his rivals. Still, he won, ahead of Brocco. In the hurly-burly, Egg and Engel had locked elbows and fallen. Octave declared himself 'as happy as a king', and, 'alone against nearly everybody' he was pleased to dedicate his victory to Monsieur Hammond. Hammond was also very pleased, paying for a large advertisement to mark this 'considerable success, this latest magnificent triumph.' In the euphoria, Lapize also told the journalists that the sun had been unbearable, of course, but unbearable for everyone. He added that it was a great pity the Pyrenees had proved his undoing, but that he was feeling ready for some more stage wins.

And then he said no more.

Nothing else was heard from Lapize because he disappeared in Nice, just before the Alps. It was a typical Lapize exit: a clean break, without any fuss, but not spotless. Desgrange wrote:

> Of Lapize, there is not much to say. We have become used to seeing impulsive behaviour from this rider each year.

Everyone took their lead from Desgrange, writing and repeating that, 'in the 1914 Tour, Octave Lapize made his inglorious exit in the Alps.' In fact, this was not the real story at all. In Nice, on 14 July, Octave was crushed by the news of his mother's death. He left immediately for Villiers-sur-Marne without feeling the need to involve the press in his personal affairs. In a show of solidarity, the La Française team pulled out of the race with him.

The Tour continued without Lapize, of course, but for the first time its popularity was rivalled by that of the big boxing matches. When the Tour arrived in Grenoble on 16 July, all eyes were elsewhere: it was the day Georges Carpentier became champion of the white world, beating Gunboat Smith inside the distance. And then more stormclouds began to gather overhead for the riders – as well as for the European heads of State on high alert in their capitals – as champions stooped to committing some most unbecoming fouls. Defraye 'arranged' his abandonment, while Faber, of all people, was caught hanging on to a car.

This should not detract from the fact that Philippe Thys won his second victory in the Tour de France, beating Henri Pélissier by just one minute and 40 seconds.

On 16 July in the Parc des Princes, the champions were welcomed with great rejoicing. During the laps of honour, the band of the 76th Infantry Regiment accompanied the laps of honour with a rousing march. And then, without anyone knowing why, or perhaps it was just a feeling, the atmosphere changed. The festive tone gave way to a more solemn one. The drums and bugles of the Légion de Paris began to play *Aux Champs* (To The Battlefield), the salute that accompanies military honours ceremonies. At the Parc des Princes, the music was changing.

So was the world.

This was the start of a confused period when the trivial went hand in hand with the deadly serious. The threat of war was felt everywhere. The French President Poincaré was on a diplomatic mission to St Petersburg, but back in Paris they were cheering Félix Mayol to the rafters of the music hall just like in the old, carefree days.

On 28 July, Austro-Hungary, pressured by Wilhelm II's Germany, declared war on Serbia which was backed by Russia, a French ally. But, on the very same day, in *L'Écho des Sports*, Victor Breyer's mind was concentrating exclusively on what the Tour should look like in 1915, in the light of the experience in 1914. Can this really have been the most pressing concern? Breyer was not the only one escaping from reality. On 30 July, believe it or not, there was a revenge match for the Tour de France at the Buffalo track. The poster announced an American-style race of 100 kilometres, where road and track champions would ride in pairs. Two well-known American pistards won the event, but no-one really cared. Lapize, with Berthet, came in third. No-one cared about that, either. Their hearts were not in it, and anyway the stands were half empty.

The time for dreaming was over.

On 31 July, Jean Jaurès, the 'apostle of peace' was assassinated at the Café du Croissant in the heart of Paris. On 1 August, Germany declared war on Russia. Octave Lapize would have followed events all the more carefully after the horrific accounts of the last war he had heard in his youth. In Villiers-sur-Marne, he could not have avoided hearing about the ferocious battles (3,000 French soldiers killed in a single day on 2 December 1870) which had ended in its occupation by the Würtemberg troops of the Kaiser's army. In any case, on 1 August 1914, Octave Lapize signed and sealed his last will and testament.

On 2 August, it was war. The walls of Paris and throughout France were plastered with posters ordering general mobilization of the army and the navy. Octave's diary entry for this date forlornly reads 'Race in Berlin'.

On 3 August, Henri Desgrange jumped onto the frenzied, vengeful bandwagon of majority opinion. He published an angry, hate-filled editorial in *L'Auto* that he personally considered as a call to defend humanity. In his excess, the director of the Tour de France surpassed himself.

Here are some extracts from his long article entitled *The Big Match*:

> My dear lads! My treasures! Lads of France! Lend me your ears!
>
> The Prussians are bastards. You've got to take them, the bastards. You have to take them. Most of all

because if you don't, they'll have you. And when they get you, you will be no more than machines obeying orders: you will be forced to salute foreign uniforms... You will not be allowed to make eyes at the ladies... You will not be allowed to have a laugh and a joke. The newspapers you read will be ordered to march to their tune. And you will have to read everything in (horrors!) German – Molière, Racine, Voltaire... That brute Kaiser Bill will send all his cops, heavies and henchmen to kick you up the backside...

It's a really big match this time, and you've got to win: make use of everything the Frenchman has at his disposal. You're not afraid of playing a tactical game, are you? You make a dummy run, then come back... You know all this better than I do, lads: it's what I've been teaching you for nigh on 15 years. But watch out! When your rifle-butts are on their chests, they will beg for mercy. Don't be taken in. Be pitiless. You have to finish off these evil imbeciles who have been trying to stop us from living, loving, breathing and being happy for the last 44 years... They will be made to understand that Alsace and Lorraine are French territory...

Ah! What a sigh Humanity will heave if you are victorious! It all depends on you, my lads! My treasures! My lads of France! We won the first round in Iena [the Battle of Iena in 1806]; they won the second in Sedan [1870]. The decider is yours if you want it, as the French can want something if they want it enough.

Was Octave Lapize aware of this article? In the 'big match' that had been announced, he was in an offside position: having been declared unfit for military service, his presence was not required in the mobilization. This must have put him in an awkward position at a time when the papers – particularly

L'Auto and *Sporting* – were publishing news about sportsmen who were at the front. At the same time, François Faber, who was not even a Frenchman but a Luxembourger, went to great lengths to get into the Foreign Legion.

Octave Lapize was not around, it seemed. In fact, he was doubtless a patriot, although certainly not spoiling for a fight. It is just that he was busy, and the reason is about to become clear.

On 14 August, he took the plunge. He enlisted and was allocated to the 19th Squadron of the Army Service Corps, automobile division, at the staff headquarters of General Foch.

Four days later, he was signing a different register, at the town hall of the 18th *arrondissement* of Paris, to declare that 'On the seventeenth of August nineteen hundred and fourteen, at half-past six in the evening at 5, Boulevard Barbès, a female child, Yvonne Germaine, was born to Octave Lapize and Juliette Augustine Clémentine Peyrot, of 11 Rue Amboise-Paré.'

There was nothing mysterious about the address 5, Boulevard Barbès: this was the home of the midwife who had delivered the baby.

The soldier Octave Lapize was a delighted and attentive father. He even had firm views on how infants should be brought up. Yvonne had to have a wooden cradle and a freer system than the traditional tight swaddling clothes. Just days after her birth, Octave noticed two small spots in the baby's left eye. Later, Yvonne told me herself that, 'It seems that he put me in his car, which had not yet been requisitioned, and took me to the Lariboisière Hospital. They told him it was nothing serious. But the funniest thing is that when I visited that same hospital 15 years later, a doctor showed me a record of my father's appointment. And if you look carefully, you can still see those little spots.'

Coming back to the war, it was surely a great advantage for Lapize and his young family for him to be stationed in Paris.

But Octave was bored in the Service Corps. The example of some of his cycling colleagues who had become pilots, and his own predilection for flying (remember his initiation just before the finish of the 1910 Tour) led him to request a transfer to the 'fifth service', as the airforce was known at the time.

On 10 September 1915, Octave Lapize was posted to the Military Aviation Centre at Avord, near Bourges. Sergeant Lapize was a particularly talented flier, as the base Commander, Lieutenant-Colonel Henry, did not fail to recognize, because on 8 October he undertook his first flight as an instructor. From the moment of his new posting, we are able to follow Octave day by day by consulting his 'schedule', a veritable logbook: 24 October 1915, first flight with a passenger; 14 March 1916, first night flight with shared command. He clocked up 211 hours and 35 minutes in a Farman, and 130 hours 10 minutes in his Nieuport. Curiously, both these types of aeroplane, each bearing the name of its inventor, were designed and built by men – Farman and Nieuport – who had been racing cyclists at the turn of the century.

Sergeant Lapize was also given leave from time to time (Yvonne heard from her mother that airmen received more than other servicemen): he was back in Paris on 18 October 1915 and, more surprisingly, in July 1916 to take part in a race at the Parc des Princes, alongside Berthet and Deruyter. No doubt it was a race 'for fun' following which, if you believe the newspapers, 'the trio showed that the war has not diminished our sporting excellence.'

Octave Lapize had managed to take his bicycle with him. We know this, because every so often he sent off to his shop (always in return for an invoice!) for the parts he needed: sometimes a chain, sometimes an inner tube. One day, he let Juliette know that he was running short of cash 'and that he needed her to send some,' remembers Yvonne. 'So, guess what. Mum just popped me in a washing basket, which made a nice cradle, and off we went to see Papa. There was even a General there who gave my cheek a pinch, saying "That's a lovely little girl you've got there, Lapize".' Yvonne remembers every detail of the stories her mother had told her later, much later, when she was old enough to understand.

But then Sergeant Lapize decided he had had enough of being an instructor. At his own request, he left Avord on 30 November 1916. He had trained 130 pilots, and was given a glowing recommendation by his commanding officer: 'Very good instructor. Plenty of drive. Perfect conduct.' He also received a diploma from the Chief Inspector of the military academies, 'in recognition of the true worth of the service rendered to the nation by its modest and courageous instructors. The instructors who are leaving for the front can be proud of their work, which will have contributed, in the hour of France's greatest need, to the formation of an airforce which is the envy of the world.'

Drill Sergeant Lapize had decided to go to the front. To prepare himself for combat missions, he first stayed at the school for aircraft gunners in Cazaux, in December 1916. In January 1917, he moved on to a placement at the school for aerial combat in Pau, where he was introduced to formation flying and aerobatics. In February, he was posted to the Bar-le-Duc region, where he began his military career, first in N504 Squadron, then in the N203.

On 24 May 1917, Sergeant Lapize arrived at N90 Squadron, based in Toul, under the command of Lieutenant Pierre Weiss. The squadron's planes were emblazoned with the silhouette of a 'crowing rooster in profile' on their fuselage. Now, Octave Lapize was at war.

He did his job well, receiving a mention in dispatches for 'saving, with a masterstroke, a single-seater escort plane in an extremely tight corner.'

On 28 June, he put an enemy plane out of action, which fell, crippled, behind its lines.

On 8 July, he made a demonstration flight for officers on a tour of inspection.

On 10 July, he was on short leave in Paris. The military information bulletin published daily in *L'Auto* described him as being in good health.

On 12 July, all flights from Toul were suspended due to bad weather, so Lapize took his bike to visit some friends from N77 Squadron, at their base 20 kilometres away. 'Just to keep myself in training,' he told them. One of his friends describes the scene:

> He was really happy as he told us about how he had shot down his first Hun. He really had shot down a plane but, unfortunately, because of the altitude, the wind had taken it back behind the lines by the time it fell, too far away to be an official kill. But the champion wasn't put out, and told us it wouldn't be long before he brought down another one inside our lines. He left us in the evening, full of beans, and our last sight of old Lapize was of a figure bent over his handlebars as he sped up the hill with no apparent effort, and disappeared over the top.

On 14 July, the anniversary of his mother's death, Octave Lapize took off on a new mission. Flight Sergeant Boillot reports the details: 'He left to chase a biplane which was being tuned up in the region of the Mortmare woods in the Woëvre. He found the Boche at around 4,500 metres and engaged it immediately. He launched two attacks from behind and, as he dived, fired 280 cartridges. On the third run, he was seen closing on the enemy, no doubt for a better aim. At that moment, the unlucky man must have taken a burst of machine-gun fire right in the chest from the Boche gunner, because his machine immediately went into a tailspin, falling several hundred metres before a wing broke off and the glorious 'Tatave' crashed to earth eight kilometres from our lines. At the autopsy they found five bullets in his body, one of which had sliced into his heart.'*

On Saturday 14 July 1917, around 7:30am, Octave Lapize was no more. N90 Squadron was cruelly plunged into grief.

The news was announced in Paris the next day at a cycling event at the Parc des Princes. On 16 July, the tributes flooded in from all directions, and were printed in newspapers throughout France.

The mention in dispatches (no.155 of the 8th Army) was published on 17 July:

> Octave Lapize, an excellent pilot of unrivalled daring and bravery, having courageously engaged two enemy fighter planes, was killed on 14 July 1917, using more than three hundred cartridges in the attack.
>
> Signed:
>
> Commander in Chief of the Eastern Armies, General Pétain
> Commander of the Eighth Army, General Girard

17 July also saw the funeral of Sergeant Octave Lapize, who had died for his country at the age of 30. Octave Lapize his father managed to reach Toul in time for the funeral. He heard from all sides that his son had been 'well loved by his comrades, who admired the fine pilot, his bravery and his

---

* The sincerity of Sergeant Boillot's account is beyond all doubt, as is his honesty. But the reliability of eyewitness accounts is always open to question. The offical version of the engagement (which took place, after all, at an altitude of about 5,000m), reported by the Squadron Leader and recorded in the dispatch, is quite different: Octave Lapize confronted not one, but two enemy aircraft. It is worth noting that observation aircraft were often escorted by several fighter planes.

sense of duty.' There were two speeches by the graveside. The one by Lieutenant Weiss is particularly moving:

> N90 Squadron has just lost one of its bravest men, whose very name stands out in all our memories, as a reminder of great performances and victories. Lapize fell in the very fiercest combat, after spending all his ammunition, fighting to the bitter end with the persistence and courage that were so familiar and natural with him, but wrapped in such modesty and simplicity that you had to see them in action to appreciate them. An airman of magnificent virtuosity, who would have been one of our greatest fighter pilots, Lapize had sworn to crown his champion's colours with new glory. Death came upon him at the moment when, leaning over his sights, fully aware of duty and danger, he launched an attack on two enemy aircraft.
>
> We are mourning a brilliant pilot and a heart of gold, and we know that in the smallest village of France, amongst those who remember having seen Lapize pass by in a cloud of dust, there will be friends and unknown admirers joining with us in our sorrow.
>
> Adieu, my dear Lapize. Sleep in peace close by your airfield. We will watch over you and protect you with our wings. Your comrades will never forget you.

Sergeant Boillot was also present at the funeral service:

> Infantry soldiers gave the last honours. The crowd drifted slowly away, leaving a few sportsmen to pay their last respects. There were four of us: Gaudermer, the footballer and racing driver; the rugby ace Boyau, the famous cyclist Miquel, and me. We left the Toul military cemetery as the gravediggers began their mournful task.

Over the days to come, the tributes and testimonials continued to pour in. Racers and cycling clubs wrote to the newspapers to express their admiration and their sorrow. The Commander of the Avord training centre named one of the avenues at his base after Lapize. Lieutenant Weiss decided to send Sergeant Lapize's second plane to the GDE crew pool near Paris, for the training of young pilots. On the side of the aircraft's cabin, which also bore the number four (the number worn by the champion in the 1910 Tour de France), he had the following lines painted:

> *Whoever you are, do not climb into this cockpit*
> *without a thought for its brilliant pilot,*
> *gloriously fallen on the field of honour.*

As usual, Juliette – companion of Octave, mother of Yvonne – was discreet in her grief. Her reaction, unusual for the era, was to write to the *Argus de la Presse* (press cuttings agency) in order to keep a written record of her partner's death. It is of great interest to read through these newspaper cuttings. At one end of the range is the sober reporting of *Le Figaro*: 'The airman and road race champion Lapize has been killed in aerial combat by an enemy bullet. Octave Lapize was an airforce sergeant.'

At the other are the wild imaginings of *L'Heure*:

> Lapize, like so many of our champions, has gone to a simple, heroic and most beautiful death, dying as only he could: assailed at 4,000 metres by a flock of Boche crows, fighting 15 against one as is their wont.

In between is a splendid piece of comment in *L'Intransigeant*:

> He was a star of the Vel' d'Hiv and the other French tracks; his name was splashed across the billboards in huge letters like that of Caruso outside the Opera. This hero will be sadly missed in the humblest seats of the velodromes.

Most remarkably of all, there are also tributes to the dead man in the foreign press, paying their own respects to his memory.

The Daily Mail wrote: 'Octave Lapize, the famous French cyclist who held the 100-kilometre road championship in 1911, 1912, 1913 and became a sergeant in the Flying Corps, has been killed in an aerial engagement.'

The New York Herald: 'Octave Lapize killed. Octave Lapize, the famous French cycle champion, who has been serving his country as an aviator, has just been killed.'

But life went on and so, even, did cycle racing. Thus, in the month of August, *L'Auto* celebrated a victory for Henri Pélissier in Trouville-Paris, after a magnificent race. Life has a way of picking itself up and carrying on from where it left off.

In November of 1917, the family managed to bring Octave's body home to the cemetery in Villiers-sur-Marne. But it was not until 1922 that the official internment ceremony took place, reported without frills in the press:

> The little church of Villiers-sur-Marne was much too small to contain the friends and admirers of the late lamented Lapize, our former French champion and one of the finest athletes that France has ever produced. The whole of Villiers was there side by side with the good Lapize senior, the champion's widow, and his family. A stately, solemn mass was sung. The body rested before the altar in its coffin, draped in the tricolour flag. Other flags, tied with black crepe, hung on all sides. The congregation listened in contemplative, sorrowful silence. The casket was surrounded by local schoolchildren, former soldiers, and ladies from the Red Cross, at the foot of which were left great piles of wreaths and sprays sent by the riders, Octave Lapize's former comrades, L'Auto, La Française, Alcyon, and the young people of the Villiers-sur-Marne cycling club. Especially prominent

was a wreath from the riders themselves, carried by Trousselier.

The congregation included the Deputy Mayor Monsieur Gorce, Brocco, Sérès, Frau Egg representing her husband, Lucien Josse from the Paris Cycling Union, Monsieur Martin, Director of La Française, and Ludovic Feuillet from the great firm Alcyon. In the cemetery, several speeches were made in the pouring rain, which only added to the ceremony's sad atmosphere. Then, deeply moved, the mourners filed past the tomb of this great champion of yesteryear, who died for his country.

In the same day's edition of *L'Auto*, an advertisement declared that, 'For the big races of 1922, the young champion Grassin will be riding a Lapize cycle with red head tube, equipped with Dunlop tyres.' It appears that the name of Lapize was showing no signs of fading away.

The brand name was indeed set to last, but the memory of Lapize himself would very soon grow dim. You can just about make out his trace in *The Finest Sports Stories* published after the war (at 60 centimes for the lot), whose author Jean Bordeaux celebrates the merits and virtues of the champion 'Labize' as he triumphs over his rival 'Laber'. And his memory just survives to merit a couple of mentions in 1930.

Yvonne Lapize was 16 that year, she recalls, when she fired the only gunshot of her life, to start a race at the Vel d'Hiv' (this, no doubt, was the Prix Dupré-Lapize, which would remain a fixture until the velodrome's demolition in 1959). The same year, the Côte de Bruyères – the main feature of the French championship circuit at Montlhéry – was renamed the 'Côte Lapize'. And then, for decades to come, hundreds of thousands of cyclists – racers and tourers alike – would tighten their clips with Lapize toe-straps, still available today. Furthermore, the company Poutrait-Morin – later Zefal – which in 1925 had acquired the rights to the Lapize brand for certain cycling accessories, received an enquiry from Argentina in 1947 about the recognition value of the name Lapize, exploring the possibility of exploiting the brand in South America. The French Federation, in a letter from its president Joinard, gave a very encouraging response. The newspaper *L'Équipe*, which had taken over from *L'Auto*, provided an unenthusiastic testimonial in a letter from its administrator M. Patrice Thominet (the absence of any comment from Jacques Goddet is most surprising).

And that was that.

* * * * *

How are we to understand the survival of the Lapize brand, while Lapize the man was forgotten? How is it that such a combination of champion and hero could disappear so quickly and so completely from our collective memory?

The first explanation is that the 1914-18 war produced a deep and brutal rupture between the prewar and postwar worlds of sport: a world reserved exclusively for a population of young men. In 1919, when there was a dearth of these young men, the Tour de France counted only 65 riders at the start and 11 at the finish.

In the 1922 tribute written at Octave Lapize's funeral in Villiers-sur-Marne, it is staggering to see the words 'champion of yesteryear' used to describe a rider who had dominated cycling just a decade earlier, a man who was within three years of being an exact contemporary of Charles de Gaulle.

The second explanation is that the Lapize family, without being reclusive, always stayed in the background, even though Octave senior kept the legendary Café Lapize going until he died in 1943 – and made provision for it until 1962. Juliette Peyrot, who had never officially become Madame Lapize, laid claim to none of her late partner's glory. She looked after her daughter Yvonne's health and gave her a good education. Juliette continued to live at the flat on the Rue Amboise-Paré until her death in 1972. After being knocked over by a car while crossing the Boulevard Magenta, she reassured her loved ones on her deathbed, telling them, 'I really was on the pedestrian crossing.' Insisting on propriety to the last, Juliette was surely a companion worthy of Octave Lapize.

We have one further piece of evidence for Octave's dignity and his sense of duty: the ultimate proof of his will written on 1 August 1914, and the state of his assets in 1921.

Three years before his death, and one day before the war, Octave Lapize had decided that his daughter Yvonne should receive 75% of his fortune, while 12.5% would go to his father Octave and 12.5% to his partner Juliette, who was already the owner of the Rue Ambois-Paré appartment.

It is not my business here to record the sum of Octave Lapize's fortune, which amounted to a good few thousands of francs – and 82 centimes, according to the official deed. On the other hand, it is surprising to note, on reading this document, that on 16 July 1914 – that is, 12 days before the *Grand Départ* of his last ever Tour de France, Octave Lapize became a shareholder and joint manager of the *Brasserie Lapize Son and Titti*. Was this a mischievous wink in the direction of Lapize senior, the brewer?

When she came of age, Yvonne was invited to a branch of the Crédit Lyonnais to take possession of the deposits and investments that her father had made in her name. 'Yes, Monsieur,' confides Yvonne, 'it was an awful lot of money for a war orphan.' She said nothing about the relative value of the franc in 1914 and 1935. The Lapizes don't talk about that sort of thing.

Had anyone ever heard Octave Lapize complain? Never.

Final portrait

The problem at the end of this journey – my problem, but yours too, dear reader – is that I cannot be sure that I really know Octave Lapize.

85 years after his death, I felt the urge to dedicate a biography to him. An urge, and probably even a need, because it seems that, all my life, I have had a certain idea of Lapize.

I first knew him long before I realized, because my father was a great admirer of both champions and aviators. I had known him properly for 10 years when I wrote an article on him for *Catholic Life* in 1962. I knew him all along, because the image of the large pastel portrait presiding over the Café Lapize in Villiers-sur-Marne remained fresh in my memory: the picture of a supremely handsome Lapize in the saddle, resplendent in his tricolour jersey.*

I knew him so well that this book is not just a *biography*, but *my* very personal biography of Octave Lapize. I myself have gathered and verified all the facts that have appeared in these pages, and I can state with confidence that my account is not an inaccurate one. All the same, it is *my* account. I find its hero so fascinating, and have done for so long, that I am 'on his side', and I probably shy away from things that do not suit my case.

For example, it is a matter of regret to me that he was only 1.65m tall (5′ 5″), even though I know full well that this was the

---

* This pastel drawing was left to a club in the 12th arrondisement, and has since disappeared.

average height in his day, and that his greatness has nothing to do with his size. For another, it makes me want to pull my hair out when people call him *'le Frisé'*, and I get cross when they say 'Tatave'.

But that is not the heart of the matter. Perhaps I have let myself be blinded to the truth, or led astray by my fascination with the character of Lapize. Frankly, I do not think so. In any case, I assume that I have not.

My judgment does find support and reassurance in some very sound pieces of evidence. Among his colleagues, Lucien Petit-Breton, five years his senior, always considered that Lapize, 'thanks to his intelligence, managed more than anyone else to obtain the maximum returns from the resources he had available.' Henri Pélissier, two years younger than Lapize, recalls that Lapize had been 'a real scruff' when he first appeared on the scene. Later on, at the end of his career, he calls him 'a phenomenon'.

Other witnesses, direct or indirect, voice opinions that have the value of being more recent. In 1951, the journalist Paul Espeit drew up a league table of all the champions he had known in the journal *Route et Piste* (Road and Track). He had no hesitation in placing Octave Lapize in the number one spot, calling him, 'the greatest champion, of whom the least had been said.' Paul Espeit had been present at the start of the career of young Octave, who 'had come to La Cipale in an attempt to gain the speed and the skill he needed.' He remembers an unassuming lad, 'who did his job without seeking publicity or making any effort to get himself noticed: this is no doubt the reason that the best rider we ever had on the road – and, at times, on the track – is one of those we have talked about the very least!'

A year later, in *Sport Sélection* monthly, Albert Baker d'Isy, an eminent and respected expert, gave Octave Lapize the first place in his world ranking. He reports this anecdote of April 1952: 'The other day, in Ghent, they were celebrating the 70th birthday of Karel Steyaert [the 'Belgian Henri Desgrange']. A group of old-timers – mostly *directeurs sportifs* and journalists –

who had known Lapize agreed that the top spot should go to Lapize.'

Last of all, and deliberately so, I will quote the *hommage* to Octave Lapize that was the first to be written, by the man who was at once the most highly-respected journalist of the era, and the most privileged follower of his career: Henri Desgrange. Published in *L'Auto*, three days after the champion's death, this text represents a kind of epitaph.

To the Ace.

Now there was an ace: Octave Lapize, who has just fallen on the field of honour. I am speaking here of cycling, and not of aviation, where he had not yet made his name in official dispatches.

Crowds tend to cheer their favourite champions, not always with the necessary level of athletic discrimination. It might seem that, after 25 years of observing sport in action, people ought by now to be able to reserve their preference for those champions who genuinely display incontestable quality. But the masses are fickle and impressionable; they are not reflective enough; they are too impetuous, they act on instinct, going not for muscular quality but appearances and big effects, drawn to those whose mannerisms, language, attitudes and origins are closest to their own. Other factors come into play: each champion has around him his own tight circle of admirers and people who have been converted to his cause at random, by a chance encounter, or a shared background; because their idol has happened to favour them with an audience or a kind word.

The secret of criticism is in independence of thought and keeping a cool head. I did not like Lapize's temperament as a sportsman, and yet I declare that he was perhaps the best road racer we have had since Huret.

I do still carry with me the memories of his disappointing Tours de France: the stages in Brittany, in the Pyrenees or on the Mediterranean where the man made up his mind in just five minutes to abandon the race, to leave us high and dry, and that nothing could persuade him to reconsider his decision, neither his chances in the general classification, nor his team-mates, nor the firm that had backed him at such expense. I remember all too well that each of these withdrawals was caused by purely financial considerations, and that Lapize saw the Tour de France as a vulgar exercise in accountancy.

None of this prevents me from seeing the real, fine, great Lapize, the man who at the top of his form and when his interests were not at stake, seemed to be head and shoulders above his rivals. 'Le Frisé', as his opponents used to call him, seemed to exert a sort of fascination over them. He held sway with the qualities that make for a roadster of endurance and, more importantly, the turn of speed that made him the deserved favourite each season for the French road championship. I remember a first Tour stage from Paris to Le Havre, where the leading group had left Lapize behind after a puncture, but was still so much under his influence that it was unable to go all out to escape recapture. They could feel the shadow of Le Frisé above their heads like a kite over a young rabbit, and, flying along with mighty strokes of his pedals, he caught his rivals in less than an hour and went on to settle the matter at the finishing post.

How to account for the quality of Lapize? He had neither Christophe's courage, Faber's panache nor Egg's nimbleness: the big events were too much for his musculature, and I believe that he was only once French road racing champion. But you cannot always explain beauty, virtue, the exceptional: you can only state them.

I recall another occasion, again on the Tour de France – the one he won – when there was a disputed finish at the end of the third stage. Lapize was given third when he thought he had taken second place, at least. Standing close to me was a capable observer, who hardly knew Lapize at all, hitherto an unknown quantity. 'Don't worry!' he called. 'You are still a great rider!'

Never was this more true than at that time, when his only concern was to pedal his way to fame, and his mind was solely on the sport itself. Later on – and who can blame him for this? – he was beset by life's material preoccupations: he had domestic and business responsibilities. He gave the impression of a great thinker, reduced to drawing a salary in some Government Ministry in order to pay the bills. After that, we would only see the great Lapize when the interests of his muscles and his bank balance coincided.

What is the point of saying he was better than this rider or not as good as that one? The late greats like Faber will not turn in their graves, and the living might take offence. Although greatness is measured by comparison to others, it still exists, even when not being compared. Mont Blanc is not Mont Blanc because it is higher than the Matterhorn or Monte Rosa. It is Mont Blanc, and that's all there is to it.

Lapize remains the greatest loss that cycling has suffered during this terrible war. The speed of Hourlier and Comès will not erase the memory of Friol, and the dear recollection of François Faber will not be diminished if we rank Lapize's athletic prowess one rung above his own.

Signed: H. Desgrenier

It would no doubt be somewhat irreverent to express dissatisfaction with such a fine article by Henri Desgrenier, the pseudonym Henri Desgrange used during the war. But that is how I feel.

His title, I admit, is not in the least bland: it is magnificent. That 'ace' does not come from the Latin. It comes newly forged, still hot from military jargon – and from the airforce in particular. The official status of ace was reserved for pilots who had shot down at least five enemy aircraft. The rugby player Boyau, for instance, who came to the cemetery in Toul, was an ace, as was the famous Guynemer, the ace of aces. Desgrange is getting a little ahead of himself, then, when he addresses Lapize as an ace. I am prepared to forgive him this, as you can well imagine.

But his text is blemished by omissions, approximations and even condemnations which I find intolerable.

To write on 20 July 1917 that Lapize had not yet had his name mentioned in dispatches is unnecessarily offensive, since the press had already published his citation of 17 July.

To suggest that Lapize 'was only once French road racing champion' smacks of provocation. Wearing the blue, white and red for three years in a row was visible testament to Lapize's lasting national supremacy on the road. And finally, to claim that Lapize 'gave the impression of a great thinker, reduced to drawing a salary in some Government Ministry in order to pay the bills,' is an insult to his memory that is both petty and unfair.

Perhaps we should see this rhetorical character assassination as evidence of a love-hate relationship with the man who had so perfectly personified the ideal of 'the head and the legs'

Perhaps. But I'm telling you:

'Hands off my Lapize.'

PALMARES OF OCTAVE LAPIZE

Amateur
1906
1st Grand Prix de Villiers.

1907
Cyclo-cross Champion of France.
Champion France; 100 kilometres road race.
1st Paris-Chartres.
1st Prix Valor.
1st Stage 3 Tour de Belgium.

1908
1st Paris-Auxerre.
3rd and Bronze medal Olympic Games 100 kilometres.
1st Course du Bol d'Or (6 hours track event).
World Hour motor-paced record (distance: 82,758 kilometres).

Professional
1909
1st Paris-Roubaix.
1st Milan- Varèse.

1910
1st Paris-Roubaix.
1st Tour de France (1st stages 5, 9 10 and 14).
. 2nd Paris-Bruxelles.

1911
Champion of France.
1st Paris-Roubaix.
1st Paris-Tours.
1st Paris-Bruxelles.
2nd Paris-Brest-Paris.
9th Six Days of New York (with Vanhouwaert).

1912
Champion de France.
1st Paris-Brussels.
1st Circuit de Touraine.
1st Six Days of Brussels (with Vandenberghe).
1st Six Hours of Paris (with Georget) .
Hour record tandem-paced (50,925 kilometres).
Record for 100 kilometres tandem-paced (2hrs 2mins 3.4secs).

1913
Champion de France.
1st Paris-Brussels.

1914
1st stage 8, Tour de France.
2nd Six Days of Brussels (with Miquel).
7th Six Days de Paris (with Oliveri).

BIBLIOGRAPHY

JOURNALS (1906-1922)

L'Auto, L'Écho des sports, Sporting, La Vie au Grand Air, Miroir des Sports.
Mémoires d'E. Christophe (1923) ; *Mémoires d'H. Pelissier* (1928).
Mémoires de P. Ruinart (1937).

BOOKS

Octave Lapize, le tacticien de la route, Charles Ravaud (1912).
Le Livre d'or du Tour de France, L'Auto (1935).
Le Tour a cinquante ans, L'Équipe (1953).
Olympika, Monique Berlioux (La Table Ronde, 1964).
Le Cyclisme, Jacques Marchand (La Table Ronde, 1963).
Les Six Jours en France (Sprint International. Hors série, 1984).
Marcel Bidot, Jacques Augendre (La Maison du Boulanger, 1996).
Villiers-sur-Marne dans l'histoire, Daniel Poisson (1996).
Encyclopédie illustrée des coureurs français, Pascal Sergent
(Eechoonaar. F.F.C., 1998).